Early Intervention:
The Next Steps

An Independent Report to Her Majesty's Government by Graham Allen MP

Graham Allen MP

January 2011

KH

4/15/13

Contents

PM LETTER

Rt Hon David Cameron MP
The Cabinet Office
70 Whitehall
London
SW1A 2AS

January 19th, 2011

I have completed the Review of Early Intervention requested by the government last June and deliver it ahead of time. I hope it will be helpful that there are no requests for legislation and no requests for immediate public spending. Should you accept and act upon the recommendations not only will the life chances of so many children be enhanced but I would also expect considerable dividends to be paid to the taxpayer and government on a recurring basis.

This Review therefore makes the following recommendations:

1. The all party co-operation that has characterised this issue should continue and be actively developed. All parties should publicly accept the core message of Early Intervention, appended, acknowledge that the culture of late intervention is both expensive and ineffective, and ensure that Early Intervention plays a more central part in UK policy and practice.

2. All parties should commit to the central objective of Early Intervention to give a **social and emotional bedrock** to the current and future generations of babies, children and young people by helping them and their parents (or other main care-givers) before problems arise.

3. With the encouragement of the government, the best and most rigorously proven **Early Intervention Programmes** should be pulled together using the best methodology and science available, to promote their wider use.

4. The government should encourage 15 local **Early Intervention Places** to pioneer the programmes.

5. The government should promote an independent **Early Intervention Foundation** independently funded, to motivate, prove the Programmes above, work with pioneering Places above and raise additional long-term finance for Early Intervention from nongovernmental sources.

6. The government should take further the existing policies in this field to make sure that all children have the social and emotional capability to be 'school-ready' at five, including:

    a. A long-term plan to give all every vulnerable first time mothers who meet the criteria and want it, access to Family Nurse Partnerships.

    b. Working up a National Parenting Campaign as part of the "Big Society".

c. High-quality, benchmarked pre-school education for two-, three- and four-year olds as part of a 0-5 Foundation stage.

d. An all-party Review to plan progress towards a quality paternity and maternity settlement.

e. A more coherent series of assessments for the 0-5's to detect and resolve social and emotional difficulties before they become intractable.

A full list of the recommendations can be found at the front of the Report.

Finally, to exploit the tremendous political and financial momentum behind Early Intervention I strongly recommend that the Social Justice Sub-committee of the Cabinet swiftly issues a timetable enabling those recommendations which are accepted to go ahead without delay.

I will publish a further Report which will be delivered to you in before the summer recess exploring the use of new private sector financial instruments to fund the local roll-out of proven Early Intervention programmes to Early Intervention Places via the Early Intervention Foundation. This is a tremendous opportunity for this and future Governments to take a long-term view on tackling causes rather than symptoms, building out dysfunction and creating essential social investments with good rates of return. Countless children – who would otherwise underachieve – will be able to meet their potential and in turn become rounded citizens and above all excellent parents if the right decisions are taken now.

Good wishes in the judgements you must make.

INSERT SIGNATURE

Graham Allen MP
The Early Intervention Review Team

The Core Message on Early Intervention

Early Intervention is an approach which offers our country a real opportunity to make lasting improvements in the lives of our children, to forestall many persistent social problems and end their transmission from one generation to the next, and to make long-term savings in public spending. It covers a range of tried and tested policies for the first three years of children's lives to give them the essential social and emotional security they need for the rest of their lives. It also includes a range of well-established policies for when they are older which leave children ready to face the challenges of each stage of childhood and of passage into adulthood – especially the challenge of becoming good parents to their own children.

In spite of its merits, which have achieved increasing recognition by national and local government and the voluntary sector, the provision of successful evidence-based Early Intervention programmes remains persistently patchy, and dogged by institutional and financial obstacles. In consequences, there remains an overwhelming bias in favour of existing policies of late intervention at a time when social problems are well-established – even though these policies are known to be expensive and of limited success. Strong leadership by *all* political parties is required to overcome this bias and achieve a cultural shift to Early Intervention. A move to successful Early Intervention also requires new thinking about the relationship between central government and local providers. It also needs authoritative evidence about which forms of Early Intervention are most successful, and about their impact.

The Early Intervention Review Team 2011

Foreword

In July 2010 the Prime Minister asked me to lead a review on Early Intervention. I was glad to accept. I have a long-standing personal interest in policies to break the cycle of deprivation and dysfunction from generation to generation. I have witnessed this phenomenon repeatedly as MP for Nottingham North –the area in which I was born and grew up. This is one of the most deprived constituencies in the UK, and it has been heartbreaking to see so many children's lives and potential wasted, all the more so for knowing that it could have been prevented by small investments in the early years of those lives. Getting this wrong has impacts way beyond the individual and family concerned: every taxpayer pays the cost of low educational achievement, poor work aspiration, drink and drug abuse, teen pregnancy, criminality and unfulfilled lifetimes on benefits. **But it is not just about money – important as this is, especially now – it is about social disruption, fractured lives, broken families, and sheer human waste.**

For that is the promise of Early Intervention. A range of well-tested programmes, low in cost, high in results, can have a lasting impact on all children, especially the most vulnerable. If we intervene early enough we can give children a vital social and emotional foundation which will help to keep them happy, healthy and achieving throughout their lives and, above all, equip them to raise children of their own, **who will also enjoy well-being.**

In 2005 I became Chair of One Nottingham, the local strategic partnership for my city. Over the next four years we set out to fulfil this promise - we had a shared vision of Nottingham as "Early Intervention City" with 16 interventions to break the 0-18 cycle of dysfunction. Nottingham has done heroically on meagre funds and incredible personal and partnership commitment. But my experience convinced me that our country needed a more focused national effort. Both in Nottingham and elsewhere we were still tackling the symptoms of social problems and ignoring the causes. Huge budgets were absorbed by remedial or palliative policies and few resources were spent on preventive policies.

People of all parties had reached the same conclusion. In 2008 Rt Hon Iain Duncan Smith MP and I co-wrote the book, *Early Intervention: Good Parents , Great Kids, Better Citizens*, setting out the stall for cross-party action on intergenerational change and feeling our way towards a national strategy.

Three years later, it is clear that our country can take the next steps necessary to gain the full benefits of an Early Intervention approach. Much excellent work has been done, at both local and national level, but new and additional lines of attack are needed.

That is the purpose of this Review and no one need fear its proposals. They will not threaten any effective policies which are now in place, nor provide any excuse or rationale for cutbacks. Instead they offer sharper tools to measure and expand the rewards of Early Intervention, to improve the execution and impact of successful policies, to make more effective use of current public expenditure, and to achieve lasting cost savings in later years. The proposals will take Early Intervention to a new and higher level.

I hope readers will find *no words of blame* in this report. Everywhere I have encountered hard work, commitment, inspiration and tenacity in the cause of Early Intervention. Ministers of successive governments and officials, local councils and the voluntary sector have put huge efforts into finding new ways to give children a better start in life. So, too, have those in the frontline, including teachers, police officers, health workers, and so many others, often without recognition ,going the extra mile every working day. Above all, mothers and carers- not least in low-income families- do the best they can in tremendously difficult circumstances often without the tiny amount of help that will make all the difference

One great merit of Early Intervention is that it can help so many families under stress to fulfil their mission of giving children a secure and loving space in which to grow up. It can keep families together and save many children from the trauma of break-up and removal. When all is said and done, enabling every child to develop social and emotional capability is nothing less than what most parents routinely do for their own children.

This Report is dedicated to all those now toiling in the vineyard of Early Intervention. I hope that they especially will benefit from its new ideas. If acted on, these ideas would make a huge difference to this generation of children and all those which follow. They will also produce massive and recurring savings for the nation.

I agreed to do this report on the basis that it was part of the continuing *all-party* effort to promote a culture of Early rather than late intervention, to build the basic components of success, rather than to throw ever more money into the chasm of failure. If we are to make a change across the generations it cannot be the property of one party: it requires all voices, all governments, a whole nation to continue the attack on the causes of dysfunction and to help all our babies, children and **young people** to have a decent chance in life.

It is the most important function of a society to make sure the next generation is equipped to meet the challenges it will face. Without exception all the political parties and their leaders have been unfailingly generous and open-minded as this report has taken shape. None of them are bound by it yet all of them understand its message. The current government and the ones that come after it, of whatever political colour, must carry Early Intervention still further until real intergenerational change is achieved.

I decided early on that this review would issue two reports. This is the first. It sets out the rationale for *Early Intervention, to create the essential social and emotional bedrock for all children* to reap the social, **individual** and economic rewards. It identifies where we can build on existing government programmes, and then discovers the best proven ones, and describes the rigorous methodology and institutional arrangements, independent of government, required to make a much-needed step change in the way in which our society invests in its human potential. Although this report recapitulates some of the argument and evidence from the book by Iain Duncan Smith and me, it contains abundant new evidence and analysis. For bringing all of this together in a few short months, I am deeply indebted to **a small** Review team of officials and outside experts from the UK and abroad. As always in such reports, any credit must be shared with them but any errors are mine alone.

A second report, to be published in May, will detail the new funding options needed to resource Early Intervention. It will dovetail with this report, as it must, for policy and funding are inseparable.

All who care about realising the potential of our babies, children and young people need to work together and take the pathway to a long-term Early Intervention culture in the UK. That pathway is mapped in this Report.

Graham Allen MP
January 2011

A note on style

Many programmes and policies across the world have been given the title and kudos of "early intervention." Not all of them deserve this status. In this review, I wish to reserve the term Early Intervention to the general approaches and the specific policies and programmes which are known to produce the benefits described in the review for children aged 0 to 3, for older children 0 to 18 who will be the better parents of tomorrow. For that reason I have generally turned it into a proper name, with capital letters. In some contexts I use "early intervention" in its everyday general sense, without capitals. GA

Executive summary

Introduction

In this first report I use the term Early Intervention to refer to the general approaches, and the specific policies and programmes, which help to give children aged 0-3 the social and emotional bedrock they need to reach their full potential, and to those which help older children become the good parents of tomorrow.

The rationale is simple: many of the costly and damaging social problems in society are created because we are not giving children the right type of support in their earliest years, when they should achieve their most rapid development. If we do not provide that help early enough, then it is often too late. Here are just a few illustrations:

- A child's development score at just 22 months can serve as an accurate predictor of educational outcomes at 26 years;

- 54 per cent of the current incidence of depression in women, and 58 per cent of suicide attempts by women can be attributed to adverse childhood experiences;

- a recent authoritative study of boys assessed by nurses at age three as being "at risk" found that they had two and a half times as many criminal convictions as the group deemed not to be 'at risk'. Moreover, in the 'at risk' group, 55 per cent of the convictions were for violent offences, compared to 18 per cent of those who were deemed not to be 'at risk'.

Using our brains

Chapter 2 describes crucial areas of brain development in the first years of life, to suggest why these years might be so predictive of future outcomes. A key finding is that babies are born with 25 per cent of their brains developed, and there is then a rapid period of development so that by the age of three when they reach delete their brains are 80 per cent developed.

In that period, neglect, the wrong type of parenting and other adverse experiences can have a profound effect on how they are emotionally 'wired'. This will deeply influence their future responses to events and their ability to empathise with other people.

This is not to say that development stops at age three – far from it – but the research indicates that we need to intervene early to make sure that our children get the best possible start in life. We need to then keep supporting them throughout childhood in ways which help them reach the key milestones of social and emotional development.

The social and economic benefits of intervening early

Chapters 3 and 4 explore the social and economic benefits of Early Intervention.

Early Intervention to promote social and emotional development can significantly improve mental and physical health, educational attainment and employment opportunities. Early Intervention can also help to prevent criminal behaviour (especially violent behaviour), drug and alcohol abuse and teenage pregnancy.

What parents do is more important than who they are. Especially in their earliest years, the right kind of parenting is a bigger influence on a child's future than wealth, class, education or any other common social factor.

The economic benefits of Early Intervention are clear, and consistently demonstrate good returns on investment. One example whose benefits have been well-documented in research is the Nurse Family Partnership in the USA. This programme supports 'at risk' teenage mothers to foster emotional attunement and confident, non-violent parenting. By the time the children concerned were 15, it was estimated to have provided benefits, in the form of reduced welfare and criminal justice expenditures, higher tax revenues, and improved physical and mental health, which were over five times greater than the cost of the programme.

Intervening later is more costly, and often cannot achieve the results that Early Intervention is able to deliver. However, very little current expenditure is spent on Early Intervention in comparison to later interventions. We need to redress this imbalance.

Early Intervention Delivery - moving on

Chapter 5 explores the key themes of the first half of the report in the context of current policy and practice. It looks at how we can build on the good things that are already going on, while keeping in mind the government's stance on public expenditure and its policy agendas of decentralisation, localism and the creation of the "Big Society".

It makes a number of recommendations that are broadly aimed at making children genuinely ready for school (the meaning of which is defined in the chapter) as part of a new 0-5 Foundation Stage.

In particular, it addresses the following issues:

- increasing awareness of what Early Intervention can achieve within central government, local areas and among parents;

- increasing the effectiveness of staff such as teachers, social workers, nurses and doctors, existing policies and infrastructure;

- providing parents with the information and support they need to help their children;

- providing the data and measurement tools that we need to help identify those in need and to track progress;

- creating the right financial freedoms for local areas to pool budgets and work across agencies to tackle shared problems.

Effective programmes

Chapter 6 identifies the most effective Early Intervention Programmes and presents the calculations which have been made of their cost-effectiveness. It lists 80 programmes which fulfil this criteria, with 19 in the top category.

It uses rigorous standards of evidence, highlighting programmes on a scale, according to the strength of evidence. This is intended to be a useful tool for private, public and third sector commissioners looking at how they should best spend their money.

However, the list is not final, and never should be. The report makes clear that it must be constantly reviewed and expanded. To this end, it recommends an independent Early Intervention Foundation (described more fully below) to increase the evidence available in the UK of successful Early Intervention and to provide further examples.

This list is especially important because it will underpin a second report examining alternative funding options for Early Intervention. This report will recognise that the government is not in a position to make new large-scale spending commitments. However, it will be based on the conviction that the economic and social returns of Early Intervention are so great that we must develop models by which mainstream private as well as public investors can invest in the future of society.

Early Intervention Places

Chapter 7 acknowledges the importance of local rather than central institutions in providing the best universal and targeted Early Intervention services.

The Chief Executives from 25 local authorities have already agreed in principle (if the government so wishes) to sign up to putting Early Intervention at the heart of their strategies and to work to start to implement some of the recommendations from this report. I would suggest 15 of them form the first group of Places. Some third-sector bodies might also join this approach.

Some of these 25 areas are also Community Budget Areas, which means that they would also be able to pool the resources from different finance streams to make it easier to tackle multi-agency issues, such as families with multiple problems, where Early Intervention could have a profound impact.

I have already had discussions with Ministers indicating that several departments would wish to pursue Early Intervention agendas in partnership with specific local areas.

The Early Intervention Foundation

If local communities are to lead this pioneering effort and operate the programmes described, they must be able to act free of central government control or interference, and also to raise money from the private sector. That is the key message of chapter 8, which emphasises that this effort is organised independently from Whitehall. Central government should champion, not control, the expansion of Early Intervention.

The prime recommendation of this report is the creation of a new, independent Early Intervention Foundation. This concept is described in Chapter 8. This Foundation would be created in the first instance through private, philanthropic, ethical and local funding and it would be run by its initial funders, independently of central government. I have discussed this with many witnesses and others interested in the field (including the 10 eminent experts in this field quoted in the report) and it is clear the will and the resources are available to establish this Foundation quickly, if central government allows.

The Foundation would undertake work with four broad ambitions:

* to encourage the spread of Early Intervention;

* to improve, develop and disseminate the evidence base of what works utilising rigorous methodologies;

* to provide independent and trusted monitoring of the effectiveness of programmes; and

* to act as an honest broker between financial investors, local authorities and deliverers to make the most of alternative funding mechanisms to provide the necessary investment that Early Intervention deserves.

Final thoughts

We need to work together, effectively, to reap the benefits that Early Intervention can bring and this will require working differently, to higher standards, and with focused activity and a vigorous institutional champion. Many contributors to the report are excited by the potential for a real breakthrough on Early Intervention, but there is also apprehension that it could be delayed and suffocated. In Chapter 9 the report indicates some of the actions we need to take to make these recommendations happen[Chapter 10 anticipates my second report on alternative funding mechanisms, which will be published in the spring. This is an exciting venture which, with active Treasury and City and voluntary help, will produce new ways to finance and facilitate the essential change in culture from late to Early Intervention.

Summary of Recommendations

In order to build on the present political and financial momentum of Early Intervention my recommendations below create *no demands for new legislation and no demands for immediate additional public expenditure.*

TOP 3 RECOMMENDATIONS

I recommend that the *19 'top programmes'* identified in my report should be supported and expanded to demonstrate our commitment to Early Intervention. However, I also recommend that this list of 19 should not be regarded as exhaustive or complete: all should be reviewed and reassessed by the new Early Intervention Foundation (proposed below) before a "living list" is evolved.

I recommend that Early Intervention builds on the strength of its local base by establishing *15 local Early Intervention Places* to spearhead its development. These should be run by local councils and the voluntary sector, who are already the main initiators and innovators of Early Intervention.

I recommend the establishment of an independent *Early Intervention Foundation* to support local people, communities and agencies, with initial emphasis on the 15 Early Intervention Places.

I recommend that the Foundation should be *led and funded by non-central government sources*, including local government, ethical and philanthropic trusts, foundations and charities as well as private investors. There is already considerable interest in this. The government should champion and encourage this concept. Whitehall should neither control nor isolate the Foundation but welcome it and engage with it as a source of complementary activity and advice.

Chapter 1

1. I recommend that the nation should be made aware of the enormous benefits to individuals, families and society of Early Intervention – a policy approach designed to build the essential *social and emotional bedrock* in children aged 0 to 3 and to ensure that children from 0 to 18 can become the excellent parents of tomorrow.

Chapter 2.

2. I recommend that the nation should recognise that influencing social and emotional capability becomes harder and more expensive the later it is attempted, and more likely to fail.

Chapter 3

3. I recommend a re-balancing of the current culture of 'late reaction' to social problems towards an *Early Intervention culture*, based on the premise of giving all children the social and emotional bedrock they need to achieve and to pre-empt those problems.

4. Within that context, I recommend an essential shift to a *primary prevention* which offers substantial social and financial benefits.

5. I recommend proper *co-ordination* of the machinery of government to put Early Intervention at the heart of *departmental strategies*, including those seeking to raise educational achievement, employability, improve social mobility, reduce crime, support parents and improve mental and physical health.

Chapter 4

6. Since waiting for problems to take root before reacting costs the taxpayer billions of pounds, I recommend that we should exploit the potential for *massive savings in public expenditure* through an Early Intervention approach.

Chapter 5

7. I recommend that the United Kingdom should adopt the concept of the *Foundation Years stage, from 0-5* (including pregnancy), and give it at least the same status and recognition as primary or secondary stages. Its prime objective should be to produce high levels of *"school readiness"* for all children regardless of family income. To support this recommendation, I further recommend that all year groups should be numbered from birth, not from the start of primary school. This will help everyone with responsibilities for child development, particularly parents, to understand how the 0-18 health and educational cycle is continuous from birth and does not start on entry to primary school.

8. Since a successful Early Intervention approach requires sustainability and a long-term view, I recommend that the Secretary of State for Communities and Local Government creates a lasting, stable settlement between central and local government within *a published framework or codification of the local/central relationship*. I further recommend that this settlement be agreed by all political parties, and adhered to whichever of them are in power in central or local government.

9. I further recommend that the Department of Health and the Department for Education work together with other partners and interests to produce within 18 months one seamless *Foundation Years Plan* from pregnancy to 5 years of age: this Plan should be widely understood and disseminated in order to make the 0-5 Foundation years a reality. I recommend that this Plan is endorsed by Parliament.

10. I believe that under the government's proposed *new arrangements for local health* services, a great opportunity exists to localise Early Intervention and I recommend that one of the reorganisation's key themes should be a focus on antenatal education/preparation for parenthood, social and emotional development for the under 3's. I recommend:

- that *GP consortia* and local authorities work together to commission evidence-based preventative Early Interventions, especially in pregnancy and the first years of life.

- that the proposed new local *'Health and Wellbeing Boards'* should create integrated Early Intervention strategies based on Joint Strategic Needs Analysis at local level, share best practice and have the freedom to tie into the institutional arrangements for Early Intervention recommended below;

- that the Department of Health and the NHS further strengthen the accountability of *local Directors of Public Health* for improving social and emotional capability.

11. I recommend the formation of a broad based all-party group to explore possible means of giving British parents and babies – when resources allow – similar benefits in *maternity and paternity support* to those now enjoyed by their Swedish counterparts and their babies.

12. I recommend that the success of *Family Nurse Partnership* should be taken further, with the specific aspiration subject to the on-going DH evaluation, that every vulnerable first time young mother who meets the criteria and wants Family Nurse Partnership should be able to access it and that discussions should take place with all relevant interests on how to ensure sustained local commissioning, leadership and finance. I anticipate that this would be one of the first programmes to be funded through one of the additional funding mechanisms now under consideration which will be outlined in my second Report.

13. I recommend that future expansion of Early Intervention programmes should favour those which combine strong evidence bases with impact on crucial stages in the development of social and emotional bedrock in children, and that the present national network of Children's Centres should use such approaches, including evidence-based evaluation systems, to identify and meet the needs of vulnerable children and families. This could include programmes such as FNP. I support the proposal in the Schools White Paper that the forthcoming National College of School Leadership should provide training for Children's Centre leaders, and recommend that this should include training on social and emotional development and evidence-based Early Intervention approaches.

14. I recommend that every child has a clear *schedule of social and emotional reviews up to and including the age of 5* so that they can be put on the path to "school readiness" which many – not least from low income households –would benefit from. Accountability is confused and divided, policy is incomplete and there is an unnecessary separation between the Healthy Child Programme reviews and the Early Years Foundation stage assessments. It is timely that several external reviews are taking place. Providing they result in a regular and coherent series of assessments Government should act swiftly to ensure that the 0 to 5's are helped at the earliest and most cost effective point in their lives to develop the social and emotional bedrock upon which they can thrive.

15. I recommend that a meeting between the Local Government Association and departmental ministers is convened to iron out problems around *data sharing* at local level.

16. I recommend that we improve *workforce capability* with the 0-5s. We should:

- increase graduate-led, or even post-graduate, preschool leadership;

- ensure that all early years settings employ someone with Early Years Professional Status (EYPS) on site;

- establish a Workforce Development strategy led by the Departments for Education and Health with input from across government, to ensure that we are developing for the future enough suitably qualified candidates who wish to work with the 0-5s.

17. In the interim, I recommend that all key professionals are made aware of the importance of building on the social and emotional capabilities of babies and children and promoting and supporting good parenting, through refocused training this year and as an integral part of Continuous Professional Development

18. I recommend a new *National Parenting Campaign* as the Crown Jewel of the Big Society project, pursued with enough passion and vitality to make it irresistible even to the most jaundiced. I recommend the creation of a broad-based alliance of interested groups, charities and foundations to ensure that the public, parents, health professionals and, especially, newly pregnant women are aware of the importance of developing social and emotional capability in the first years of life, and understand the best ways of encouraging good later outcomes for their children. Whitehall departments should participate in this initiative but not control or dominate it. For this reason, I propose that this initiative should be funded and directed from outside central government. In the interim, I recommend that specific recommendations on parenting should be published as a response to the recent consultation by the Department of Health on proposals on information for patients, service users, carers and the public.

Chapter 6

19. I recommend that a greater proportion of any *new public and private expenditure be spent on proven Early Intervention policies* rather than on unproven ones.

20. I recommend that a *new rigorous methodology on evaluating* and assessing Early Intervention programmes should be instituted and developed for the UK, aimed at identifying the best, most effective programmes to help our babies, children and young people.

21. I recommend that the *19 'top programmes'* identified in my report should be supported and expanded to demonstrate our commitment to Early Intervention. However, I also recommend that this list of 19 should not be regarded as

exhaustive or complete: all should be reviewed and reassessed by the new Early Intervention Foundation (proposed below) before a "living list" is evolved.

22. I recommend that a growing number of excellent well-regarded UK programmes should be assisted in *joining the list* as proven programmes able to help our children the most..

Chapter 7

23. I recommend that Early Intervention builds on the strength of its local base by establishing *15 local Early Intervention Places* to spearhead its development. These should be run by local councils and the voluntary sector, who are already the main initiators and innovators of Early Intervention.

24. I recommend that where helpful the Places could voluntarily *link to Government Departments* where Early Intervention agendas overlap: positive preliminary discussions have already taken place with several Departments to explore this.

Chapter 8

25. I recommend the establishment of an independent *Early Intervention Foundation* to support local people, communities and agencies, with initial emphasis on the 15 Early Intervention Places.

26. I recommend that the Foundation should be *led and funded by non-central government sources*, including local government, ethical and philanthropic trusts, foundations and charities as well as private investors. There is already considerable interest in this. The government should champion and encourage this concept. Whitehall should neither control nor isolate the Foundation but welcome it and engage with it as a source of complementary activity and advice.

27. I recommend that the Foundation be given the following *roles*:

- to lead and motivate the expansion of Early Intervention;

- to evaluate Early Intervention policies based on a rigorous methodology and a strong evidence base, and encourage others to do the same;

- to advise the 15 Places and other local councils and organisations; and

- to develop the capacity to attract private and public investment to Early Intervention.

28. I recommend the *immediate creation of a 'shadow' Early Intervention Foundation* including those quoted at the beginning of the chapter to bring these proposals to fruition.

Chapter 9

29. I recommend that *all political parties* work together on the Early Intervention agenda. Even before the publication of this Review I wrote to all party leaders to ask that they continue to work – together where possible – on Early Intervention policies in the future in a way which builds on the recommendations of this Review.

30. I recommend that the Social Justice Cabinet Committee resolves the issue of future *cross-government co-ordination* on Early Intervention policy immediately on presentation of this Review.

31. As soon as ministers resolve their approach, I recommend that the commitment across government to Early Intervention should be given the strongest and most active leadership by the Permanent Secretaries Committee especially on how to join up departmental thinking and delivery on Early Intervention, and in particular how to get buy-in from local authorities.

32. I recommend that the successful interaction begun by the Review with local government should be continued and developed, especially by giving *local government* a leading role in the Early Intervention Foundation.

33. I recommend the establishment of *a transition team* to secure swift implementation of any of the key recommendations accepted by the Cabinet committee.

Chapter 10

34. A further report on the *Financing of Early Intervention* is being prepared by my team and I recommend that the Social Justice Cabinet Committee ensures that the team is properly resourced and staffed to enable the report to be presented before the Parliamentary summer recess.

Part 1: Introduction

This first half of the Report sets the scene for the policy proposals in Part 2.

1. It outlines the concepts and philosophy of Early Intervention and why we need to do more to rebalance the dominant culture of late intervention with the more effective and less expensive culture of Early Intervention. This entails direct help to children, parents and care-givers in coping with their immediate circumstances, but it also means preparing the same children to become the most effective parents they can be.

2. In Chapter 2 I examine the phenomenal growth of children's brains in the first years of life, and show how this creates exceptional opportunities, especially for mothers , to provide children with the social and emotional foundations that are the key to personal development and achievement and the best single way to tackle inter-generational dysfunction.

3. Enabling infants to become rounded, capable people results in great and lasting social benefits through a lifetime that runs from happiness and security in childhood, achievement in education, readiness for productive work and, above all, successful parenthood. This argument is made in chapter 3. But all too often we fail to achieve this, and many children never develop the social and emotional faculties which they need in life. If we continue to fail, we will only perpetuate the cycle of wasted potential, low achievement, drink and drug abuse, unintended teenage pregnancy, low work aspirations, anti-social behaviour, and lifetimes on benefits which now typifies millions of lives and is repeated through succeeding generations.

4. In chapter 4 we explore the massive structural deficit of failure, which dwarfs any public expenditure cuts and yet which we continue to pay without question. Billions of pounds are paid out year after year, indeed decade after decade, often without the faintest acquaintance with an evidence base. Although, ironically, advocates of prevention are constantly exhorted to improve their evidence base. Success or failure in early childhood also has profound economic consequences. Socially and emotionally capable people are more productive, better educated, tax-paying citizens helping our nation compete in the global economy, and make fewer demands on public expenditure. Socially and emotionally incapable people are far less likely to be productive taxpayers and far more likely to be a cost to public funds in benefits, health care, social work and policing and criminal justice.

5. I hope to demonstrate by the end of this first half of the Report that Early Intervention not only works as a concept but that it makes evident social and economic sense. Only then would it be right to ask the British government and British people to take Early Intervention to the next level.

b

Chapter 1
Early Intervention: Providing the Social and Emotional Bedrock for All Children

What you see consistently are children at a very early age are starting school already behind. That's why I've said that I'm going to put billions of dollars into early childhood education ..... Every dollar that we spend in early childhood education, we get $10 back in reduced dropout rates, improved reading scores. That's the kind of commitment we have to make early on.

Barack Obama

Introduction

1. Early Intervention enables every baby, child and young person to acquire the social and emotional foundations upon which our success as human beings depends. Most parents reading this report give this to their children, and often by instinct and common sense alone, but all of our children deserve nothing less. A child who is rounded, capable and sociable has a great chance in life. Those denied those qualities have a bad start and few of them recover. During their lifetimes they can impose heavy penalties on themselves and generate major costs, financial and social, for their families local communities and the national economy. In our book in 2008 Iain Duncan Smith and I outlined the essential philosophy of Early Intervention as a means to forestall bad outcomes for children and society, and I do not repeat this here.

2. However, it is important to set the scene in this introduction. The message remains the same: there are no quick fixes, no magic bullet, just a long -term programme of hard work. I am asking all parties and all governments, this one and its successors, to settle on a sustained policy, generation after generation, for our children. If we can do this we will not only improve current society but offer that which succeed it a new and better level of health and well-being by building this into the early lives of its youngest members.

Early and Late Intervention

3. There are now two competing cultures, one- the dominant one – of late intervention, the second- the growing one – of Early Intervention. I explore in later chapters how we can bring these two into better balance. It is not an either/ or – we *must* continue to swat the mosquitoes but we can drain the swamp too. The bleak truth is that decades of expensive late intervention have failed. Major social problems have got worse not better, despite heroic frontline efforts tackling the *symptoms* their *causes* often remain unaddressed. Little or no value for money can be demonstrated for the billions of pounds spent on current late intervention programmes and little prospect of value from the billions set aside fatalistically for such programmes in the future. It is quite right to be asked to give a strong evidence base for Early Intervention programmes (and we

do this in this Review) but the default position of spending billions of pounds over decades on late intervention should be subject to the same challenge.

4.   The central problem for all developed countries, especially ours, is that intervention happens too late, when health, social and behavioural problems have become deeply entrenched in children and young peoples' lives. Delayed intervention increases the cost of providing a remedy for these problems and reduces the likelihood of actually achieving one. More often than not, delayed intervention results only in expensive palliative measures which fail to address problems at their source. It is time to recognise that the prevailing culture of late intervention is expensive and ineffective.

5.   However, there is another way. I make clear in chapter 6 that the right type of Early Intervention programmes, those that build social and emotional capabilities, have resulted in significant and sustainable improvements in health, behaviour and social and economic outcomes. They offer immediate rewards to individuals and local communities and the prospect of lasting gains to society and the economy. Because of the huge costs of late intervention it does not take long for the right Early Intervention programmes to more than pay back their costs many times over – even on the most conservative estimates of savings which I have insisted on throughout this report. But the costs of Early Intervention are, anyway, far lower than those required for late intervention programmes. To give only one example, an independent cost-benefit analysis of life skills training estimated it could provide a 25-fold return on its initial, relatively small, investment[1].

6.   Other investments, such as early years education, have lower rates of return, but, nonetheless, have previously generated substantial savings, particularly when expressed in terms of each individual benefitting. For example, the same cost-benefit analysis found on average early years education for three to four year olds in low-income families had a benefit to cost ratio of 2.36 to 1 in the USA. Based on current exchange rates, this corresponded to a net benefit per individual of notably over £6,000.

7. The clear evidence of strong returns from Early Intervention is central to my proposed investment strategy. I return to it in later chapters and will explore it in depth in a second report in May.

Opportune Time for Change

8. More and more eminent thinkers, policy makers and practitioners are acknowledging the importance of Early Intervention in children's lives. Teachers, health workers, police officers and parents tell the same lesson. My team and I have examined hundreds of submissions to this Review. We have scanned the major reviews of social problems published over the last three years. Almost without exception, they mention the need for early intervention (as is illustrated in the boxes throughout this chapter).

9. The intellectual climate is now highly supportive of an Early Intervention approach and the political climate has shifted favourably in the last few years. When Iain Duncan Smith and I published our book in 2008, all of the current leaders of the major United Kingdom political parties gave generous and flattering endorsements to the concepts of Early Intervention which we set out."[2]

10. Our society now has a once-and-for-all opportunity to capture the immense potential rewards from Early Intervention. Many programmes with established success are ready for broader implementation, others are starting up and need help to thrive and be tested. In chapters 6 to 8 of this report I show how this help can be provided.

Part of the Big Society

11. There is also much scope for experiment and innovation in Early Intervention, and for engaging the energy and creativity of volunteers. To coin a phrase, Early Intervention is a "big society" project, which could unite public and private sectors behind achievable goals. Of course, the large public sector institutions will take the lion's share of resources but my proposal in chapter 8 for an Early Intervention Foundation, offering independent and impartial advice, has already elicited substantial interest from non-government sources.

12. I have much sympathy with the present government's general ambition to give more scope to local decision-making and voluntary engagement in public life; indeed, I argue later that this should go much further and be safeguarded from repeal. However, no one is confusing localism with atomisation, and it is essential that where appropriate local authorities work together and share costs and learning. To achieve a significant change in the provision of Early Intervention, local areas need to identify the most productive Early Intervention policies and to develop shared goals so that they can benefit from the economies of scale that arise from working together.

Financial Involvement

13. In these times of fiscal constraint, this country needs to be more imaginative about creating new mechanisms to fund investments in early intervention – and I mean investments. Underlying all the thinking in this report is the belief that Early Intervention is a means to achieve lasting gains in the human capital of our country. It would improve our international competitiveness and raise our long-term GDP. In the last few years I have been delighted to see more and more financial experts offering ideas for the financing of Early Intervention. Their contribution is crucial. My two reports will, therefore, seek to establish new opportunities for investment in Early Intervention which would appeal both to hard-headed private investors, seeking a worthwhile rate of return, and to ethical and philanthropic investors seeking to put something back into society.

14. Supplementing but not replacing government finance, such new investment would help to finance a better society for the future, one that will become less unequal and that will benefit us all socially and financially, rich and poor alike, in the longer term. At the Prime Minister's direction, work has begun to create additional statistical measures of national well-being.[3] Early Intervention has a major contribution to make in this field, and I believe strongly that such measures should be a benchmark for the social and emotional development of young children – both as an indicator of national well-being and as an agent for its improvement. I make proposals for this in chapter 5 of this report.

Real and Effective Early Intervention

15. The rewards of Early Intervention arise from establishing a healthy social and emotional development in infancy. There is abundant evidence, much of it cited in this report, to suggest that the first three years of life create the foundation in learning how to express emotion and to understand and respond to the emotions of others. Lessons learnt in that period can last a whole lifetime, and prepare an individual to progress physically, mentally and emotionally at every stage of later life – especially in becoming a good parent. That is not to say that we do not develop socially and emotionally after that stage. However, lessons not learnt in that formative period become harder and harder to learn later in life, and the longer the delay the more it sets up the individual to fail in later life – especially as a parent. Early Intervention is a long- term strategy that works across and affects successive generations. We hold in each of us not only the genetic makeup of those who come later but also the keys to their development as social and emotional beings. Early Intervention breaks the all too common cycle in which people who grow up with dysfunctional behaviours and lifestyles transmit them to their children, who, in turn, transmit them to the grandchildren. Early Intervention offers a real chance to break so destructive a pattern and of raising children to become good parents and carers in their turn. Breaking the intergenerational cycle of dysfunction and under-achievement is the greatest prize that Early Intervention can offer.

Brain Growth

16. Early Intervention is not a new discovery. It is an old adage that prevention is better than cure. The philosophy is enshrined in old folk wisdoms – an ounce of prevention is better than a pound of cure; a stitch in time saves nine; a good beginning makes a good ending. The classic public health definition of "primary prevention" refers to interventions which ward off the initial onset of a disorder, i.e. intervening before damage takes place in a way that avoids the later costs in both human and financial terms of handling the consequences of the symptoms of that damage. Primary prevention which develops a social and emotional

underpinning largely takes place before birth and in the first three years thereafter, before a child's social and emotional responses become set.

17. The early years are far and away the greatest period of growth in the human brain. It has been estimated that the connections or synapses in a baby's brain grow 20-fold, from having perhaps 10 trillion at birth to 200 trillion at age 3[4]. For a baby, this is an explosive process of learning from the environment. The early years are a very sensitive period when it is much easier to help the developing social and emotional structure of the infant brain, and after which the basic architecture is formed for life[5]. However, it is not impossible but it becomes significantly harder for the brain to develop later, particularly in terms of emotional capabilities, which are largely set in the first 18 months of life.

0-3s or 0-18s?

18. It is parents and carers who are the key agents to provide what makes a healthy child between the ages of 0-3. However, to fulfil their roles those parents and carers must themselves benefit from policies across the age range 0-18 which significantly strengthen the ability of babies, children and young people to develop the ability to raise their future children with the social and emotional capabilities which are the right of every child. These policies are also interventions, which break damaging cycles and prevent the transmission of social and emotional underdevelopment through successive generations.

19. So I do not accept the false choice that Early Intervention is either 0-3 alone or 0-18 alone. It must be both.

20. Similarly, even remedial programmes can find a place in Early Intervention if they are helping create better future parents. Interventions for these older children which attack the inter-generational nature of poor social and emotional capabilities are also a legitimate strategic target in a strategy of prevention. That is why Early Intervention encompasses later programmes which enable children to grow into young people with the social and emotional competences they need to learn and to make effective choices about life. Only by acquiring these competences themselves will they

be able to transmit them to their own children.

21. Through Early Intervention the next and succeeding generations could be prepared and made ready for school, for work, for parenthood and life itself – and a virtuous circle would replace the current vicious circle of failure. Such a strategy would also call for particular attention to be paid to children in care, young offenders and the children of offenders, since their levels of risk are so very much higher than those of their other children and young people of their age.

22. However, I must make clear that fidelity to the concept of Early Intervention cannot be stretched to include every social intervention policy currently on offer, nor can it be used as an automatic defence against the threat of public expenditure cuts. As I make clear in chapters 6 to 8 some Early Intervention programmes are more true to its approach than others, and have a much greater record of proven success.

23. To reiterate: Early Intervention may be most effective before three of age, but we also need to address those aged 0-18 so they can become the most effective parents possible for the next generation of 0-3s. The 0-18 cycle needs to be addressed over and over again until the repetition of dysfunction from one generation to another is finally broken.

24. In chapter 2 I present in more depth the scientific evidence which supports the success of Early Intervention mechanisms and the benchmarks which demonstrate achievement. However, I think it helpful now to outline in general the social and emotional capabilities which I believe to be a bulwark against the cycle of dysfunction. They are set out below in Box 1.

Box 1: Bedrock capabilities

Social Capabilities – a child will engage in give-and-take exchanges with an adult; will engage with other children; will demonstrate the ability to get along with others; will understand and respond to the emotions of others; will develop a sense of belonging to a larger community through social interactions and relationships and will have an awareness of his or her relationship to others in a group; will develop the ability to interact co-operatively with others.

Emotional Capabilities – a child has secure attachment; is able to experience, recognise and express a variety of emotions, and to recognise and empathise with those emotions in others; will manage his or her internal states and feelings, as well as stimulation from the outside world; will develop strategies to control emotions and behaviours; will manage his or her behaviour, and will recognize his or her ability to do things.

25. By building these capabilities we enable children to be happily engaged with others and with society and to learn, to fully develop, to attain and to achieve. These skills are such critical building blocks that most people would assume that they are common to all of us. Yet for many they are absent or underdeveloped. This has inevitable consequences for the individual and society. Building their essential social and emotional capabilities means children are less likely to adopt anti-social or violent behaviour throughout life. It means fewer disruptive toddlers, fewer unmanageable school children, fewer young people engaging in crime and anti-social behaviour. Early Intervention can forestall the physical and mental health problems which commonly perpetuate a cycle of dysfunction to the next generation.

26. Indeed, evidence and experience from our country and overseas suggests that Early Intervention that develops social and emotional capability can reduce truancy, anti-social behaviour, crime, health problems, welfare dependency, need for statutory social care, under-attainment,

exclusion from school, and the need for educational alternative provision. All of these problems impose enormous and continuing costs on local and national government and on wider society. Many of these costs show up in public accounts but others are invisible, although no less real to their victims. For example, one disruptive child at school can exhaust the attention and energy of teachers and reduce the quality of education for other pupils. Fear of crime can trap other people in their homes. Perhaps worst of all, poor outcomes for young people often impact on their own parenting capacity as they take on responsibility for our next generation of children. In reducing common social problems, Early Intervention offers both immediate rewards of society and the prospect of long-term gains. In our book in 2008 Iain Duncan Smith and I cited some of the evidence to support that assertion: since then that evidence has grown greater and stronger.

Adverse Childhood Experiences

27. Much academic literature clearly demonstrates that adverse childhood experiences can have a detrimental influence on a number of outcomes. The California Adverse Childhood Experiences Study (ACE)[6] was one of the largest investigations ever on links between childhood maltreatment and later-life health and well-being. As many as 17,000 participants had comprehensive physical examinations and provided detailed information on childhood abuse, neglect and family dysfunction. The study found that adults who had adverse childhoods showed higher levels of violence and anti-social behaviour (Hosking and Walsh[7]), adult mental health problems[8], school under-performance and lower IQs (Perry)[9], economic under-performance (Sinclair)[10], and poor physical health. These led to high expenditure on health support, social welfare, justice and prisons; and lower wealth creation. The scientific rationale for Early Intervention is overwhelming.

The Inter-generational Cycle

28. Largely remedial public funding, invested over generations, and repeated shifts in public policy have done little to affect a fundamental problem: those children who grow up in dysfunctional

families are more likely to themselves create such families.

29. The alternative to the inter-generational cycle of dysfunction is to use Early Intervention to create a virtuous circle. At every key point in life there are early Intervention measures, which when used together form a circle which will break such cycles illustrated in figure 1. In chapter 7 I will identify specific cost-effective programmes that have been proven to work at each stage.

30. Only by ensuring that children have this basic foundation of social and emotional skills will we be able to ensure that they are school ready, life ready and child ready, as defined in Box 2.

Figure 1

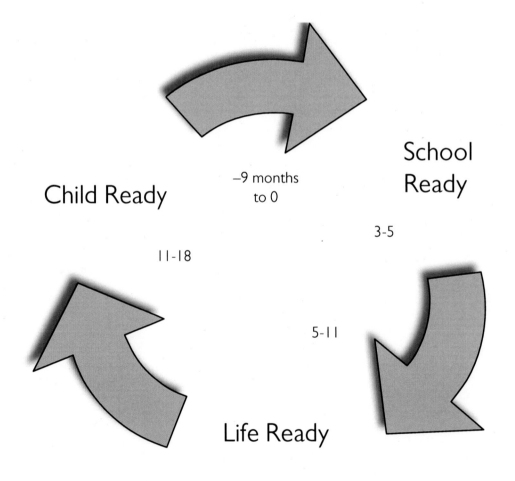

School Ready

−9 months to 0

Child Ready

3-5

11-18

5-11

Life Ready

Box 2:

School ready; having the social and emotional foundation skills to progress in speech, perception, ability to understand numbers and quantities, motor skills, attitude to work, concentration, memory and social conduct, have the ability to engage positively and without aggression with other children and ability to respond appropriately to requests from teachers

Life ready; having the social and emotional capability to enter the labour market, understanding the importance and social, health and emotional benefits of entering work, the impacts of drug and alcohol abuse, crime and domestic and other violence

Child ready; having an understanding of what it is like to build and sustain a relationship, to have a family and look after a small child, of how babies grow and develop and how parents can best promote this development.

How This Report Proceeds

31. In Chapter 6 I include a virtuous circle of interventions covering a generation aged from 0-18 and on to the next generation. They all have a strong evidence base to suggest their ability to arrest passing dysfunction and disadvantage from one generation to the next.

32. However, I recognise that it is not enough to clarify how Early Intervention works. I also need to address the financial and institutional barriers that have checked, even blocked, its progress on the ground. I have already suggested that Early Intervention has to compete with established budgets for unavoidable "late intervention" programmes. But it also has to overcome the institutional interests of established agencies which deliver these programmes, often with specific targets. In chapters 3 to 5 I explore these economic and structural problems.

33. In chapters 6, 7 and 8 I suggest what is needed to create the right institutional arrangements to ensure that central government, local authorities, the voluntary sector, and parents and carers work together to achieve better outcomes for our children and society.

Recent policy changes at national level provide an ideal opportunity for local authorities and other policy makers to make a step change in how they approach and join up early intervention provision at local level.

For example, a Pupil Premium to support the disadvantaged children, was announced in July 2010

The Comprehensive Spending Review, published in October 2010, also announced:

An Early Intervention Grant to support children at greatest risk of multiple disadvantage

Community Based Budgets to allow local areas to pool resources to support families with multiple problems

All disadvantaged two year olds to be given 15 hours per week of free education

A recruitment drive to create a further 4,200 health visitor posts.

Summary of Recommendations

Chapter 1

34. I recommend that we should be aware of the enormous benefits to individuals, families and society of early intervention.

Endnotes

1   S. Aos, R. Lieb, J. Mayfield, M. Miller, & A. Pennucci. (2004) Benefits and costs of prevention and early intervention programs for youth. Olympia: Washington State Institute for Public Policy, Document No. 04-07-3901

2   Allen, G and Duncan Smith I. (2008) "Early Intervention: Good Parents, Great Kids, Better Citizens" London: Centre for Social Justice and the Smith Institute

3   The National Wellbeing Project, Office for National Statistics, November 25th, 2010, http://www.ons.gov.uk/about/consultations/measuring-national-well-being/index.html

4   Huttenlocher, P. R. 1984. Synapse elimination and plasticity in developing human cerebral cortex. American Journal of Mental Deficiency 88:488-496.

    Huttenlocher, P.R. and Dabholkar, A.S. (1997). Regional Differences in Synaptogenesis in Human Cerebral Cortex, Journal of Comparative Neurology, 387, 167-78.

5   National Scientific Council on the Developing Child (2004). *Young Children Develop in an Environment of Relationships: Working Paper No. 1*. Retrieved from www.developingchild.harvard.edu

6   Anda RF, Felitti VJ, Walker J, Whitfield, CL, Bremner JD, Perry BD, Dube SR, Giles WH. (2006). The Enduring Effects of Abuse and Related Adverse Experiences in Childhood: A Convergence of Evidence from Neurobiology and Epidemiology. *European Archives of Psychiatry and Clinical Neuroscience*; 256:174-86 (E-pub: 2005; Nov 29)

7   Hosking, G.D.C. and Walsh, I.R. (2005). The WAVE Report 2005: Violence and what to do about it. WAVE Trust, Croydon

8   Anda RF, Felitti VJ, Walker J, Whitfield, CL, Bremner JD, Perry BD, Dube SR, Giles WH. (2006). The Enduring Effects of Abuse and Related Adverse Experiences in Childhood: A Convergence of Evidence from Neurobiology and Epidemiology. *European Archives of Psychiatry and Clinical Neuroscience*; 256:174-86 (E-pub: 2005; Nov 29)

9   Perry, B.D. (1995) Incubated in Terror: Neurodevelopmental Factors in the Cycle of Violence. In J.D. Osofky (ed.) Children, Youth and Violence: Searching for Solutions. Guilford press: New York.

    Perry, B.D. (2001). The neurodevelopmental impact of violence in childhood. In D. Schetky & E. Benedek (Eds.), Textbook of child and adolescent forensic psychiatry. Washington, DC: American Psychiatric Press.

10 Sinclair, A. (2007). 0-5: How Small Children Make a Big Difference. Provocation Series 3, No 1. The Work Foundation, London

Chapter 2
Using our brains

...a lack of appropriate experiences can lead to alterations in genetic plans. Moreover, although the brain retains the capacity to adapt and change throughout life, this capacity decreases with age[1].

Thus, building more advanced cognitive, social, and emotional skills on a weak initial foundation of brain architecture is far more difficult and less effective than getting things right from the beginning[2].

Introduction

1. This Chapter sums up the science behind early intervention, highlighting the influence on children's social and emotional development of the ante-natal, early years and later years environments. For a broader look at this topic see 'Early Intervention: Good Parents, Great Kids, Better Citizens'[3]

2. Science illustrates that well-meant attempts to understand and tackle social problems have often failed because they have taken little account of the fact that children's early experiences lay the foundation for their future development. This is a fundamental issue: the way people respond to situations is rooted in their early years, a time when they rarely have contact with social service agencies unless there are very significant problems in their lives, often resulting from parental mistreatment.

3. Our responses to situations are not pre-set at birth. The nature/nurture debate has moved on, as was demonstrated in *Early Intervention: Good Parents, Great Kids, Better Citizens*[4]. To establish the right environment for those aged 0-3 environment is to seize the earliest, the best and

most inexpensive chance to have an impact on a child's development and, therefore, improve social capability and emotional capacity.

The innate drive to social and emotional health

4. Children are born with an instinct to engage socially and emotionally, especially with their mothers. They communicate with the voice, face and hands. They express a curiosity both about the world and their need for comfort and security. There is evidence that complex dynamic social emotions, including "pride", "shyness" and "showing off", are felt and expressed by infants, with a powerful effect on others[5].

5. The emotions in the exchanges between mother and baby have been tested by observing what happens when the response to a baby's interest is blocked or fails. For example, if a mother holds her face still for a minute during face-to-face play with her two-month-old, the infant turns away and shows distress[6]. A similar pattern of anxiety and sadness appears when the mother presents the uncommunicative manner of simulated depression. Real post-natal depression interferes

with the infant's communication and cognition and, if it persists, is accompanied by limited cognitive development in later months[7]. An unhappy, unresponsive adult carer limits a baby's ability to develop its social and emotional capabilities.

Early experiences determine brain architecture

6. A baby's early experiences are influential in determining the course of his or her future emotional, intellectual and physical development. Children develop in an environment of relationships beginning (usually) within their family. From early infancy, they naturally reach out to create bonds, and they develop best when caring adults respond in warm, stimulating and consistent ways. This secure attachment with those close to them leads to the development of empathy, trust and wellbeing. In contrast, an impoverished, neglectful, or abusive environment often results in a child who doesn't develop empathy, learn how to regulate its emotions or develop social skills, and this can lead to an increased risk of mental health problems, relationship difficulties, antisocial behaviour and aggression.

7. While almost all parents want to do the best they can for their child, many find this very difficult, especially when there is interplay between such factors as poverty, mental ill health (including post-natal depression), addiction and violence in the family.

8. The importance of the quality of relationship in this early period is described by the Harvard Center on the Developing Child:

"Just as in the construction of a house, certain parts of the formative structure of the brain need to happen in a sequence and need to be adequate to support the long-term developmental blueprint. And just as a lack of the right materials can result in blueprints that change, the lack of appropriate experiences can lead to alterations in genetic plans. Moreover, although the brain retains the capacity to adapt and change throughout life, this capacity decreases with age.

The exceptionally strong influence of early experience on brain architecture makes the early years of life a period of both great opportunity and great vulnerability for brain development. An early, growth-promoting environment, with adequate nutrients, free of toxins, and filled with social interactions with an attentive caregiver, prepares the architecture of the developing brain to function optimally in a healthy environment. Conversely, an adverse early environment, one that is inadequately supplied with nutrients, contains toxins, or is deprived of appropriate sensory, social, or emotional stimulation, results in faulty brain circuitry. Once established, a weak foundation can have detrimental effects on further brain development, even if a healthy environment is restored at a later age."[8]

Secure attachment

9. Deep, long-lasting, emotional attachment influences mind, body, emotions, relationships, and values[9] and has a positive effect on self-esteem, independence, the ability to make both temporary and enduring relationships, empathy, compassion, and resiliency.

10. People who are comfortable with others, willing to depend on them and value and are comfortable with intimacy are said to have secure attachment. People who have doubts about others, cannot make relationships, shy from intimacy and aren't very trusting are said to have avoidant attachment. Those who want to get close to others but have apprehensions about rejection are said to have anxious attachment.

11. Research has long shown that people with an insecure attachment are more likely to have social and emotional difficulties. For example, some forms of insecure attachment are associated

with significantly elevated levels of perpetrating domestic violence (Dutton et al, 2006); and higher levels of alcohol and substance abuse; and having multiple sexual partners (Walsh, 1992; Brennan and Shaver, 1995).

12. Recent research also shows insecure attachment is linked to a higher risk for a number of health conditions, including stroke, heart attack and high blood pressure (McWilliams, L. 2010) and suffering pain, for example from headaches and arthritis. Secure attachment was not linked to any health problems studied.

13. Huntstinger and Luekhen (2004) showed that people with secure attachment show more healthy behaviours such as taking exercise, not smoking, not using substances and alcohol and driving at ordinary speed.

The role of the mother's mental state

14. Sensitive and responsive care, and the psychological availability of the carer, result in secure attachment. Research shows that adults who are best able to reflect upon their own experiences coherently, and who can best understand the motivations guiding the behaviour of their parents and themselves, are the most likely to have babies who are securely attached[10].

15. In looking at the incidence of impairments to the development of social and emotional capability, we must, therefore, look for factors reducing the ability of parents, and especially mothers (as they tend to be the main caregivers), to respond sensitively to the needs of their babies.

Causes of impairments to children's social and emotional development

16. Some submissions to the Early Intervention Review drew attention to the parental behaviour predictive of later childhood problems. A children's centre in Tower Hamlets observed that two thirds of its current (2010) case load contains exhibit some or all of the following:

- poor bonding
- social isolation
- negative behaviour management

- poor parenting skills
- post-natal depression of the mother, and
- lack of stimulation of the child

17. There is wide consensus that warm, attentive, stimulating parenting strongly supports children's social, emotional and physical development.

When the environment is impoverished, neglectful, or abusive, this often results in a child who doesn't develop empathy, learn how to regulate their emotions or develop social skills and this can lead to an increased risk of mental health problems, relationship difficulties, anti social behaviour and aggression.

18. Parents who are neglectful, depressed (or suffering other mental disorders), or who are drunk, drugged or violent, will have impaired capacity to provide this social and emotional stability and create the likelihood that adverse experiences might have a negative impact on their children's developmental risks as they mature. Although poor parenting practices can cause damage to children of all ages, the worst and deepest damage is done to children when their brains are being formed during their earliest months and years. The most serious takes place before birth and during the first 18 months of life when the part of the brain governing emotional development is identified to be taking place. The antenatal period is as important as infancy to the outcome for a child because maternal behaviour has such strong impacts on the developing foetus. As well as the danger of Foetal Alcohol Spectrum Disorder, which is the leading known cause of

intellectual disability in the Western world , prenatal exposure to alcohol has been associated with developmental delays and behavioural problems. Psychosocial stress during pregnancy has been linked to increased risk for ADHD, schizophrenia and social abnormalities.

Importance of mental health

19. Research now shows that mental health problems often have their roots in early childhood and, happily, there are methods, based on evidence, to make a big difference there.

20. To quote the Royal College of Psychiatrists (October 2010):

"There is no health without mental health… vast evidence that mental illness is associated with a greater risk of physical illness – and physical illness in turn increases the risk of mental illness. It's clear that strategies to improve the health of the nation will only be effective if they address mental health and wellbeing as well.

"Tackling mental health problems early in life will improve educational attainment, employment opportunities and physical health, and reduce the levels of substance misuse, self-harm and suicide, as well as family conflict and social deprivation. Overall, it will increase life expectancy, economic productivity, social functioning and quality of life. It will also have benefits across the generations."

Causes of mental disorder

21. There is wide consensus that complex disorders such as mental illnesses are based on the interaction of numerous genetic and environmental factors. Compelling evidence suggests that adverse childhood experiences – abuse, neglect, loss of a parent or drug and/or alcohol addiction in the home – are major risk factors for the development of mood and anxiety disorders (as well as physical disorders and drug/alcohol/tobacco consumption).

The importance of the infant brain

22. Flexibility in sculpting the infant brain has enormous survival value, enabling infants to adapt to environment (Shore, 1997). Different parts of the brain (governing, for example, sight, hearing etc) develop in different sensitive windows of time. The estimated prime window for emotional development is up to 18 months, by which time the foundation of this has been shaped by the way in which prime carer interacts with the child. (However, emotional development, especially emotion regulation takes place throughout childhood, and there is a further reorganisation during early adolescence.) Studies show maternal depression is a prime factor in determining behavioural problems for many children (Shaw et al, 2003) and impedes brain development (Ounce of Prevention Fund, 1996). Infants of severely depressed mothers show reduced left lobe activity (associated with being happy, joyful and interested) and increased right lobe activity (associated with negative feelings) (Dawson et al, 1994). These emotional deficits are harder to overcome once the sensitive window has passed.

23. Studies have also found a link between low maternal responsiveness at 10-12 months to aggression, non-compliance and temper tantrums at 18 months; lower compliance, attention-getting and hitting at two years of age; problems with other children at three; to coercive behaviour at four and fighting and stealing when the child is six (Shaw & Winslow, 1997). Low maternal responsiveness at 18 months did not seem to have this effect (Martin, 1981), consistent with the hypothesis that windows for development make the timing of deprivation– that period when it takes place – significant.

Infant trauma

24. If the predominant early experience is fear and stress, the neuro-chemical responses to those experiences become the primary architects of the brain. Trauma elevates stress hormones, such as cortisol[13]. One result is significantly fewer synapses (or connections). Specialists viewing CAT scans of the key emotional areas in the brains of abused or neglected children have likened the experience to looking at a black hole. In extreme cases the brains of abused children are significantly smaller than the norm and the limbic system (which governs the emotions) may be 20-30 per cent smaller and contains fewer synapses.

25. High cortisol levels during the vulnerable years of 0-3 increase activity in the brain structure involved in vigilance and arousal (the locus coeruleus, responsible for hair-trigger alert), as one might expect in a child under the permanent threat of sudden violence (Eisler and Levine, 2002; Perry et al, 1996). For such a child the slightest stress unleashes a new surge of stress hormones, causing hyperactivity, anxiety and impulsive behaviour.

26. The peak age for child abuse in the UK is 0-1[14], during precisely the period when the infant brain is most vulnerable, and when social and emotional bedrock is being put in place – or not.

Attunement and empathy: keys to healthy emotional development and non-violence

27. Schore (2000) has spoken of "the child's first relationship, the one with the mother, acts as a template… [that] permanently moulds the individual's capacity to enter into all later emotional relationships".

28. To attune to a child means responding to its emotional needs, resulting in the child's sense of being understood, cared for and valued. Empathy begins with the sense of oneness with the other created in this process of attunement. The quality of empathy – the ability to feel for and with another – is not only key to building sound emotional stability, it is also a key inhibitor of the development of propensity to violence. Conversely, empathy fails to develop when prime carers fail to attune with infants in the first 18 months of life. Absence of such parental attunement, combined with harsh discipline, is a recipe for violent, anti-social offspring. Empathy is influenced very early in life by observed parental reactions to another's suffering. Even in their first year, children already show signs of whether their reaction to the suffering of another is empathy, indifference or downright hostility.

Lack of attunement – starting down the road to dysfunction

29. Sadly, for many parents attunement either does not come 'naturally' (because they did not receive the benefit of it themselves), or is disrupted by post-natal depression, domestic violence or other severe stresses. If a child does not experience attunement, its development is retarded, and it may lack empathy altogether (check reference Sroufe or Stern)

30. The presence or absence of the sound foundation of emotional development has significant implications for levels of physical, emotional and mental health, individual achievement, and violent crime. A baby who is healthily attached to its carer can regulate its emotions as it grows older because the cortex, which exercises rational thought and control, has developed properly. Conversely, when the life of a child has been badly impacted, the cortex is underdeveloped – and the damaged child lacks an "emotional guardian". The negative outcomes can include depression and other mental disorders, and committing violence and child abuse in later life – thereby perpetuating the negative family cycle.

31. Much of the focus of this chapter has been on social and emotional development and the early years. This is not to say that we cannot amend attitudes and abilities later in life. However, as has been pointed out in chapter 1, influencing social and emotional capability becomes much harder and more expensive the later it is attempted.

32. The brain does retain some degree of plasticity throughout life, although at a much lower level and, of course, knowledge, skills and opportunities can mediate against some negative effects.

Summary

33. The case, then, is for early intervention programmes as a means to help *all* children acquire the social and emotional foundation they need. Most children acquire at home, but many do not. Intervening early to help that group helps all children develop and achieve. In this chapter we have attempted to present the overwhelming scientific evidence that the first years of a child's life are essential to the development of its brain and, especially, its social and emotional capabilities. This development depends vitally on a baby's formation of a close and trusting bond with at least one main carer. Failure to develop such a bond can have dire

lifelong consequences, both for individuals and societies. Unless and until we recognise the way major problems are formed early in people's lives, no amount of well-intentioned policy or initiatives will succeed in reducing them.

Kraamzorg is a universal post-natal service provided in the Netherlands (through a compulsory health insurance system) in the first eight to ten days after the birth of a baby. Kraamzorg aims to aid the recovery of the mother and provide her with advice and assistance to care for her newborn. The National Guidelines for Postnatal Care categorise kraamzorg in three levels: Basic level support covers:

* care for mother and baby

* regular health checks (for example, that stitches are clean and healing, the uterus is shrinking)

* advice and instruction (hygiene, feeding etc)

* ensuring hygiene levels are high

* basic household chores which directly relate to the care of mother and baby

* support to integrate the newborn into the family

For more needy families a more comprehensive level of support is provided. In this case care may extend to looking after other members of the household (like other children) and additional household tasks not directly associated with the mother and newborn.

While the maternity nurse is looking after the mother she keeps a special diary called a *kraamdossier* to make notes about the health and progress of the mother and baby. This book is used for reference by the doctor, district midwife, health clinic and others.

When the nurse is due to leave she informs the district nurse at the health clinic, who will then be responsible for continuing help and support. The health clinic is responsible for providing routine healthcare and checking the development of children from birth until they start primary school at the age of four.

The consultatiebureau (mother and well-baby clinic)

Following on support after birth, there is a well established network of clinics where families can have their babies' growth and development monitored, and receive advice on issues concerning feeding, sleeping, growth and stimulation, or any problems which may arise. Approximately 97 per cent of families make use of this service.

Summary of Recommendations

Chapter 2

34. I recommend that we should recognise that influencing social and emotional capability becomes harder, is more expensive and is less likely to succeed the later it is attempted.

Endnotes

1 Keuroghlian, A.S. & Knudsen, E.I. (2007). Adaptive auditory plasticity in developing and adult animals. *Progress in Neurobiology*, 82, 109-121. Buonomano, D.V. & Merzenich, M.M. (1998). Cortical Plasticity: From Synapses to Maps. *Annual Review of Neuroscience*, 21, 149-186. Karmarkar, U.R. & Dan, Y. (2006). Experience-dependent plasticity in the adult visual cortex. Neuron, 52, 577-585.

2 Knudsen, E.I., Heckman, J.J., Cameron, J.L., & Shonkoff, J.P. (2006). Economic, neurobiological, and behavioral perspectives on building America's future workforce. Proceedings of the National Academy of Sciences, USA, 103, 10155-10162.

3 Allen, G. and Duncan Smith, I. (2008) *Early Intervention: Good Parents, Great Kids, Better Citizens*. London: Centre for Social Justice and the Smith Institute

4 Allen, G. and Duncan Smith, I. (2008) *Early Intervention: Good Parents, Great Kids, Better Citizens*. London: Centre for Social Justice and the Smith Institute

5 Murray, L., & Trevarthen, C. (1985). Emotional regulations of interactions between two-month-olds and their mothers. In T. M. Field & N. A. Fox (Eds.), Social perception in infants (pp. 177-197). Norwood, NJ: Ablex.

Trevarthen, C.(1998) The concept and foundations of infant intersubjectivity. In Braten, S.ed. *Intersubjective Communication and Emotion in Early Ontogeny*. (Cambridge: CUP)

6 Tronick, E., Als, H., Adamson, L., Wise, S., & Brazelton, T. B. (1978). The infant's response to entrapment between contradictory messages in face-to-face interaction. *Journal of Child Psychiatry*, 17, 1-13.

7 Murray, L., Cooper, P. (1997) *Postpartum Depression and Child Development*. New York, NY: Guilford Press.

Tronick, E.Z. & Weinberg, M.K. (1997). Depressed mothers and infants: Failure to form dyadic states of consciousness. In L. Murray, & P. Cooper (Eds.), *Post Partum Depression and Child Development*. New York: Guilford Press

8 Keuroghlian, A.S. & Knudsen, E.I. (2007). Adaptive auditory plasticity in developing and adult animals. *Progress in Neurobiology*, 82, 109-121. Buonomano, D.V. & Merzenich, M.M. (1998). Cortical Plasticity: From Synapses to Maps. *Annual Review of Neuroscience*, 21, 149-186. Karmarkar, U.R. & Dan, Y. (2006). Experience-dependent plasticity in the adult visual cortex. *Neuron*, 52, 577-585.

9 Levy T.M. (2000) editor. *Handbook of Attachment Interventions*. USA: Academic Press

10 Fonagy, P., Steele, M., Steele, H., et al (1991). The capacity for understanding mental states: the reflective self in parent and child and its significance for security of attachment. *Infant Mental Health Journal*,12(3):201-18.

Bosquet, M. and Egeland, B. (2001). Associations among maternal depressive symptomatology, state of mind and parent and child behaviors: implications for attachment-based interventions. *Attach Hum Dev*

11 Lancet. 1986 Nov 22;2(8517):1222. PMID 2877359

12 Abel, E.L., & Sokol, R.J. (1987). Incidence of fetal alcohol syndrome and economic impact of FAS-related anomalies: Drug alcohol syndrome and economic impact of FAS-related anomalies. *Drug and Alcohol Dependency*, 19(1), 51–70. PMID 3545731

13 Gunnar, M.R., Donzella, B. (2002). Social regulation of the cortisol levels in early human development. *Psychoneuroendocrinology*, 27(1-2):199-220.

14 Department for Children, Schools and Families (2009) *Referrals, assessments and children and young people who are the subject of a child protection plan, England - year ending 31 March 2009*. DCSF. Tables 3B, 3C and 4A., Available online at www.dcsf.gov.uk/rsgateway/DB/SFR/s000873/index.shtml

Data Unit Wales (2009) Gwion: Data Unit Wales Dissemination Tool.

Available online at http://dissemination.dataunitwales.gov.uk [accessed 6 Oct 2009]

Select: Personal Social Services (PSS)>Children>Performance management (PM1)>Children and Young Persons on the Child Protection Register.

Chapter 3
Early Intervention: Good for People

"if I had the choice between a thousand health visitors or thousand police officers I'd choose the thousand health visitors every time"

Chief Supt John Carnochan, Strathclyde Violence Reduction Unit.

1. The first two chapters established that a child whose life is set from the beginning on a positive pathway through nourishing and nurturing in early life is more likely to have an interest in life and learning, to treat his or her fellows well and to grow to be an adult, who contributes both socially and financially to society.

2. This chapter looks at the importance of early development to subsequent outcomes and the contribution that Early Intervention can make to resolve these issues. We briefly set out the benefits of intervening earlier rather than later, and the evidence that demonstrates whether or not we are achieving effective Early Intervention policies.

How much can society benefit from Early Intervention?

3. In previous chapters, and in *Early Intervention: Good Parents, Great Kids, Better Citizens*, we have illustrated the negative influence of adverse experiences on the infant brain and the subsequent negative effects in terms of crime (especially violent crime), poor examination results, higher rates of teenage pregnancy, lower

rates of employment, higher rates of depression and suicide and later substance abuse.[1,2]

4. The findings from a number of studies suggest that early experiences are important, even after we allow for those other factors that we know are important determinants of life chances. For example, The Effective Provision of Pre School Education (EPPE) study highlights just why we need more focus on the early years. The study concludes that the quality of a child's relationships and learning experiences in the family have more influence on future achievement than innate ability, material circumstances or the quality of pre-school and school provision, and that what parents do is more important than who they are.[3] This conclusion was backed up in a comprehensive review on the evidence of parenting[4] and by Waldfogal and Washbrook, who also concluded that parenting behaviours played a significant role even after controlling for a varied set of demographic characteristics.[5]

5. The importance of getting things right in the early years is also well documented from research conducted on the Millennium Cohort Study. A child's development score at just 22 months can

serve as an accurate predictor of educational outcomes at when he or she is 26. These studies illustrate just how important Early Intervention is for future achievement and why the government has been right to invest more in better quality provision for younger children. Early Intervention needs to be at the heart of education, work and social mobility policies.

6. To take another example, the ACE Study (previously cited in chapter 1) estimates that 54 per cent of current depression and 58 per cent of suicide attempts in women can be attributed to adverse childhood experiences[6]. Poor maternal mental health is subsequently linked to poorer outcomes. Early Intervention will have a positive effect on the mental health of the nation and must therefore be at the heart of mental health strategies.

7. However, the positive effects of Early Intervention are even more wide reaching. Farrington and West[7] found that aggressive behaviour at the age of eight predicts the following when the subject is 30 the age of 30: criminal behaviour, arrests, convictions, traffic offences (especially drunk driving), spouse abuse and punitive treatment of one's own children. The Dunedin Study[8] further explores this, noting that those boys assessed by nurses at the age of three as being "at risk" had 2½ times as many criminal convictions as the group deemed not to be at risk. In addition 55 per cent of the offences were violent for the "at risk" group, as opposed to 18 per cent of those not "at risk". Early Intervention will have a positive effect on reducing crime and, therefore, must be at the heart of crime strategies.

Early Intervention helping the next generation

8. The necessary focus on the early years should not distract from the fact that there are, of course, important things that we need to do for our older children especially when the first opportunities have been missed to ensure that we break dysfunction being passed from one generation to the next.

9. A recent review of the literature on brain development agreed that the early years of the brain's development were foundational, but made, however, a case for continued support throughout life. Neurological and biological changes in adolescence mean that teenagers become more interested in sensation seeking (with a link to substance abuse and sexual desire) and the most frequently used neural pathways are strengthened and the less frequently used die off. These findings underscore the importance of close and careful nurturing of teenagers – in particular by parents – through experience and opportunity.

10. A number of programmes are suitable for this age group and will help develop better parenting for the next generation.

11. We look in more depth at the programmes and systems that have been shown to work throughout the text, but particularly in chapter 6 where we focus on those programmes for which there is strong evidence.

12. The types of interventions are wide and varied – sometimes universal and sometimes highly targeted. We can help our children by building better attunement and the development of empathy, by showing interest in our children and using rich and positive language, by supporting maternal mental health and discouraging substance abuse, we help our children. To take just one example, it is possible to engage vulnerable parents and improve the home learning environment[9] and this is not just part of what should be expected of the mother alone. Children whose fathers are involved in their learning do better at school and have better mental health, even after other factors such as fathers' socio-economic status and education have been taken out of the equation[10].

The benefits of early versus late intervention

13. As the next chapter will illustrate, people who have had adverse early childhood experiences can end up costing society millions of pounds through their lifetimes, both in direct spending to cope with their problems and behaviours and in the indirect loss of output and tax revenues from themselves and those they affect.

14. It is more cost-effective to tackle problems earlier, because it is easier to succeed, and because if we tackle them later they are likely to escalate and intensify. If a child has one or two early adverse experiences it increases the risk that he or she will have more of them. This is known 'The Accentuation Principle'.[11]

15. In 1995 Caprara and Rutter drew attention to the impact on vulnerability of adverse early life experiences.[12] They found that almost all psychosocial adversities tend to have their greatest impact on those who are already psychologically vulnerable; moreover, their effect is to increase or accentuate those pre-existing predispositions or characteristics.

16. However, the converse is also true. James Heckman, the Nobel Prize-winning economist, explains the much higher financial return from investment in children in the earliest years of their lives as due to the principles that "learning begets learning" and also "good behaviour begets good behaviour".[13] A virtuous circle is established, instead of a vicious downward spiral.

17. The wisdom of stepping in before downward spirals begin is

18. well recognised in the field of health. A policy statement by a recent US Surgeon General, said:

> "Preventing an illness from occurring is inherently better than having to treat the illness after its onset"[14].

19. This statement referred to the classic public health definition of primary prevention which wards off the initial onset of a disorder.

20. Early Intervention is both inherently better and inherently cheaper than late intervention. Unfortunately, policy practices in the UK over the past half century or more have not recognised the sound principles of this strategy. Almost without exception, UK policies for the care of children in the social, emotional and mental health spheres are based on the principle of waiting until matters go seriously wrong, and then intervening with too little, too late. Even in physical health, where some primary prevention takes place, many of the early life causes of later ill-health are ignored or neglected.

Are We Achieving Successful Early Intervention?

21. The NSPCC estimate that 13% of children have suffered some form of abuse whilst 2% suffer some form of neglect during childhood[15].

22. There were 603,700 referrals to children's social services in 2009 -2010. Yet a survey in 2009 of two London boroughs showed that 80 per cent of referrals to children's services were not even investigated. This ratio is probably not untypical of many local authorities.

23. But even when action is triggered, is it effective? One London borough's experience suggests not. Croydon's primary care trust and local authority carried out a joint assessment of the total public spending in the borough[16]. They found that parents often did not feel their holistic needs have been heard or met. Even the best provision did not address needs in a systematic manner. Liaison between agencies was inadequate, and attention was focused on "delivering services"[1] and not on "meeting families' needs"[2]. Staff commented that there was insufficient time to listen (especially to pick up mental ill health issues); that the people who need services the most often do not or cannot gain access to them; and that systems are too reactive and do not effectively anticipate problems in families. One manager stated: "You can't believe the level of unidentified need coming into children's centres."[3] Early warning signs in children and families received no response.

24. The Croydon assessment also found that engagement with services was often ad hoc and "by luck". There were large gaps — sometimes of years - between noticing problems, referrals and interventions. It showed that money was directed towards services and not solutions. Funding was allocated to budgets on the basis of historic levels, not on what would make a difference.

25. The assessment identified the biggest weakness of the traditional (and typical) systems as a significant gap between what was needed and what was offered in preventative services and Early Intervention up to age three. What early years' services there were had little or no continuity of care or continuity of relationship built into them. Most contacts with children and families

served a very narrow purpose (e.g. babies were just weighed and measured, with no attention to their holistic needs). Services tended to focus on provision rather than problem-solving, were often focused on one area of need, and were not tenacious enough with families who were chaotic or not coping. Another manager, having analysed where money was being spent in the borough, commented: 'We found it nearly impossible in most cases to link investment to outputs, let alone outcomes.'[4]

The United Nations Office on Drugs and Crime (UNODC) and World Health Organisation (WHO) have set up a Global Initiative on Primary Prevention of Substance Abuse, declaring the primary prevention approach – acting before young people begin using substances – is key for responding to substance use among young people.

The WHO strategy on Chronic Respiratory Diseases is founded on a platform which includes primary prevention to reduce the level of exposure of individuals and populations to common risk factors.

In 1998 WHO called for a global commitment to primary prevention of mental illness, stressing that this was not just a matter for medical professionals, but that vital preventive work can also be carried out by lawmakers, government departments, police, administrators, voluntary organisations and many others.

The 2005 WHO World Report on Violence and Health draws attention to the need for investment in primary prevention as one of its main recommendations. It points out that to succeed this will require an array of interventions including legal reforms, strengthening of social protection services, education and advocacy

26. **The Alternative** Current approaches are neither timely nor effective. This report calls for a paradigm shift away from the failed policies of late reaction, which have produced the catalogue of problems outlined in chapters one and two, to a new approach of investment in primary prevention.

27. Sweden's recent experience offers some relevant lessons. Sweden applies the principle of primary prevention widely in its approach to early years. In the last 20 to 30 years, Sweden has recognised the value of prevention and Early Intervention programmes and increased investment in them.

28. Other countries are following Sweden. The Netherlands recently adopted a primary prevention strategy with their policy "Every Opportunity for Every Child". This specifically stated that evidence from Sweden and other countries showed that offering parental support to all young parents as an integral part of youth healthcare reduced the incidence of child abuse. The Dutch policy statement, which puts great emphasis on protecting children and supporting parents in the first four years of a child's life, says that prevention is the goal of all interventions.

29. As far back as 1998 the World Health Organization recognised that with the right social and emotional bedrock established at the beginning of their lives children are much more easily steered to a positive path for the rest of their lives.

30. A shift to a primary prevention strategy in the UK is essential to underpin all other recommendations in this report. We shall continue to waste billions of pounds unless and until we base all policy on the premise that all children should have the best start in life. Giving them their essential social and emotional foundations is not only right in principle, as recognition of their basic human and legal rights, but also makes the best possible fiscal and economic sense for the country as a whole. Such an approach is increasingly gaining popularity and, indeed, the present government has announced a variety of policies which recognise the importance of Early Intervention, albeit sometimes with little resources.

31. In chapter 5 we further explore the policies that will be required for our services to shift to an Early Intervention strategy.

Recommendations – Chapter 3

32. I recommend that there should be a re balancing of our late reaction culture towards an early intervention culture, tested against the measure that every child should have the social and emotional bedrock they need to achieve.

33. I recommend that a shift to a primary prevention strategy to help produce the social and financial benefits evident in this chapter , is essential.

34. I recommend that proper co-ordination of the machinery of government will ensure that Early Intervention should be at the heart of departmental strategies including those hoping to raise educational achievement, employability, improve social mobility, reduce crime, support parents and improve mental and physical health.

Croydon Council and NHS Croydon used their Total Place pilot to undertake an innovative deep dive review **into the journey from conception to age 7 from both their services and families perspective**. As a result they have generated significant breakthroughs in their shared understanding of the problems and challenges inherent in their children and families' system. They have also identified opportunities to support families more effectively and key places where they can obtain much better value for taxpayers' money.

Their vision for the future, which includes a significant shift in investment and activity towards prevention and early intervention work, includes:

• Geographically based Family Engagement Partnership Teams, focussed on shared outcomes for families from conception for the first three years

• An Early Years Academy for integrated training and delivering evidence based interventions

• The Croydon Family Space web service.

In this model, Preparation for Parenthood and Find me Early approaches will transform the way services respond. For example, Family Engagement Partnerships will recognise the wider needs and vulnerabilities of mothers who would be directed to social networks for support. Early warning signs such as missed appointments would be followed up. Particular care would be taken with the most vulnerable parents, such as teenagers in particular, with the Family Nurse Partnership. The system would be set up with the capacity to spot and respond early and quickly to needs in areas such as attachment, motor skills, emotional or behavioural issues, speech and language, maternal mental ill-health and domestic conflict. Appropriate services would be available for referral; identification and response would take place long before children were believed to be at risk. Any gaps in childhood development before a child starts school would be addressed.

Endnotes

1   Lanius R and Vermetten E 9eds (2008), The Hidden Epidemic: The Impact of Early Life Trauma on Health and Disease, Cambridge University Press.

2   Allen G and Smith I-D (2008), Early Intervention: Good parents, Great Kids. Centre for Social Justice and the Smith Institute.

3   Sylva K, Melhuish E and Sammons P (2004), The Effective Provision of Pre School Education (EPPE) Project: Findings from Pre-School to the End of Key Stage 1. Institute of Education, University of London and University of Oxford.

4   Desforges, C with Abouchaar A (2003), The Impact of Parental Involvement, Parental Support and Family Education on Pupil Achievement and Adjustment: A literature review. DFES Research report No. 433.

5   Waldfogal, J and Washbrook, E. (2009), Income-related gaps in school readiness in the US and UK. Appam Fall research Conference.

6   Anda RF, Felitti VJ, Walker J, Whitfield, CL, Bremner JD, Perry BD, Dube SR, Giles WH. (2006). The Enduring Effects of Abuse and Related Adverse Experiences in Childhood: A Convergence of Evidence from Neurobiology and Epidemiology. European Archives of Psychiatry and Clinical Neuroscience; 256:174-86 (E-pub: 2005; Nov 29)

7   Farrington. D, Coid. J, Harnett. L, Jolliffe. D, Soteriou. N, Turner. R, West. D, 2006, Criminal Careers up to the Age of 50 and Life Success, Home Office Research Study 299.

8   Dunedin Multidisciplinary Health and Development Study (April 1972).

9   Evangelou, M. Sylva, K. Edwards, A. Smith, T. (2008), Supporting Parents in Promoting Early Learning: The Evaluation of the Early Learning Partnership Project, DCSF Research Report 039

10 Flouri, E & Buchanan, A. (2001) 'Father time'. Community Care, 4-10 October, 42 2001

11 Elder Jr G.H. and Caspi, A. (1990). Studying lives in a changing society: Sociological and personological explorations. In A.I. Rabin, R.A. Zucher and S. Frank (eds) Studying persons and lives, 201-247. New York, Springer Verlag

12 Caprara, G.V. and Rutter, M., (1995). Individual development and social change, in: Rutter M. and Smith D.J. (Eds) Psychosocial Disorders in Young People; Time Trends and Their Causes: J. Wiley: Chichester.

13 James J. Heckman & Dimitriy V. Masterov, (2007), "The Productivity Argument for Investing in Young Children," NBER Working Papers 13016, National Bureau of Economic Research, Inc.

14 United States. Public Health Service. Office of the Surgeon General (1999). Mental Health: A Report of the Surgeon General. Washington, DC: National Institute of Mental Health Available at: http://www.surgeongeneral.gov/library/mentalhealth/chapter2/sec5.html

15 Cawson, P., Wattam, C., Brooker, S. and Kelly, G. (2000) Child maltreatment in the United Kingdom: a study of the prevalence of child abuse and neglect. London: NSPCC

16 NHS Croydon & Croydon Council, (2010), Child: Family: Place: Radical efficiency to improve the outcomes of young children.

Chapter 4
Early Intervention: Good for the Economy

Right here in Birmingham, there are two notorious gang families who have cost taxpayers £37 million. What an appalling waste. It doesn't have to be this way. Council spending on Early Intervention for children and families can deliver £10 of savings for every pound spent. Investing money to address the causes of social breakdown is far more effective than subsidising the symptoms. So we'll allow councils to pool the budgets across the public sector – social services, care, housing and health improvement – and reward councils for delivering results and preventing social breakdown.

The Right Honourable Eric Pickles MP, Secretary of State for Communities and Local Government, speech to the Conservative Party conference, 3 October 2010

1. The earlier chapters showed that there are large social benefits to intervening early, for example in terms of improvements in behaviour, reduction in violent crime, higher educational attainment, better employment opportunities, and more responsible parenting of the next generation. They also demonstrated that failure to intervene early can create more problems later on, which are more expensive to cope with and difficult, or impossible, to remedy.

2. This chapter moves on to look at the economics of Early Intervention, specifically to examine what we are spending now and the economic case for spending more. We then discuss how we can evaluate if specific programmes are effective.

Low spending on Early Intervention

3. Current levels of UK expenditure on Early Intervention are low. Indeed, national estimates[1] have put prevention spending at four per cent of total health spending. Within this, primary prevention accounted for just 1.4 per cent of total health spending.

4. At the local level, a recent HM Treasury report on the Total Place pilot area studies[2] noted that, while 'individuals and families with complex needs impose significant costs on areas, in most cases they are not tackled through targeted, or preventative activities[3]'. A recent detailed analysis by North-West NHS found prevention was just 4% of their total spending.[4] In their joint Total Place report Croydon's PCT and local authority commented[5]: 'despite a growing consensus in the UK that prevention is demonstrably better than cure, ...a significant shift in investment from picking up the pieces to Early Intervention and

prevention has not occurred'. They go on to describe a pattern which seems typical of local authorities across Britain – of systems which are too reactive, of problems not effectively anticipated, of interventions which take place too late and with too little effect. Budgets are largely allocated on an historic basis, not by reference to what would achieve the best outcomes. Systems are designed to deliver services, not to change outcomes. Croydon concluded that one of the biggest flaws in their existing systems was 'a significant gap in prevention and Early Intervention up to age 3'.

5. Indeed, the OECD has recently reported that "country spending profiles examined are not consistent with the theory and evidence on child well-being. In contrast there is little or no obvious rationale for why so many Governments place the weight of their spending on late childhood".

6. The OECD argues that spending on young children is more likely to generate more positive changes than spending on older ones, and indeed, is likely to be fairer to more disadvantaged children. But they note that in the UK, for every £100 spent on early childhood (0 to five years), £135 is spent on middle childhood (6 to 11 years) and £148 is spent on late childhood (12 to 17 years)[6].

7. This is not a cost-effective way of treating society's problems. We acknowledge, of course, that some services will remain important in later life, but we must start to invest resources much earlier in life. Our second report will look at some alternative funding options which could give society the opportunity to provide new support to those grappling with acute social problems and use saved resources from endless, expensive later intervention programmes (which typically are less effective) towards investing more in cheaper, more effective Early Intervention programmes.

The economic case for Early Intervention

8. There is a wealth of evidence that Early Intervention policies can offer excellent returns for both individuals and local communities which can be sustained and multiplied on a larger scale. In this section we describe the economic case for Early Intervention in more detail.

9. To determine whether Early Intervention strategies and programmes are more economically beneficial, whether to the taxpayer or private investor one must take into account the following factors:

- The current and projected costs of the problems which the chosen Early Intervention programmes are intended to address.

- The current and projected costs of the existing programmes which are directed at the problems.

- The probability that these problems will diminish or disappear if existing programmes continue, or in the absence of any intervention whatsoever.

- The projected costs of Early Intervention programmes as replacements for existing programmes, including practical costs associated with integrating new forms of intervention into current public, private and voluntary structures.

- The probable impact of Early Intervention programmes on the problems concerned.

- The projected cost of the problems remaining after Early Intervention programmes have been implemented.

10. Put another way, it is necessary to make economic comparisons between three scenarios: doing nothing at all, continuing with existing policies, and replacing those policies with Early Intevention policies. Using in each case the likeliest assumptions about outcomes, each scenario offers a different mix of costs or savings. If the Early Intervention scenario offers a better savings than either of the others it represents a worthwhile investment. A growing body of evidence suggests that this is precisely the case. Studies based on highly conservative estimates of the impact of Early Intervention policies have suggested that they can generate excellent returns on the investments required to establish them.

The returns on investment

11. The returns from intervening early have been well documented[7]. We have not had time in this review to create new analyses, but we can present some examples of the returns that have been reported from a selection of well-regarded studies.

12. For example, an evaluation by the Rand Corporation of the Nurse Family Partnership (a programme targeted to support '"at risk" families by supporting parental behaviour to foster emotional attunement and confident, non-violent parenting) was estimated to have provided savings for high-risk families by the time children were aged 15. These savings came in the form of reduced welfare and criminal justice expenditures and higher tax revenues, and improved physical and mental health over five times greater than the cost of the programme.[8]

13. An independent review has placed the average economic benefits of early education programmes for low-income three and four year-old at close to two and a half times the initial investment: these benefits take the form of improved educational attainment, reduced crime and fewer instances of child abuse and neglect[9]. Within this overall figure, there is substantial variation, and reviews of individual early education programmes recorded benefit-to-cost ratios as high a $17:1[10].

14. Returns have also been demonstrated in smaller projects, as such projects adapt to the fact that they need to be more cost-effective than others in order to attract investment. For example, a joint venture by PCTs and 12 children's centres in Blackpool led to an increase in breastfeeding rates of 16%, with an estimated return of £1.56 for every £1 invested, and estimated savings to the Department of Health of £57,700 over a two-year period[11].

15. Some of the largest returns have been seen in improving children's ability to communicate, something central to any child's social development. It has been estimated that the benefits associated with the introduction of the literacy hour in the UK, even after controlling for a range of other factors outstrip the costs by a ratio of between £27:1 and £70:1.[12]

16. In addition, different areas are doing their own evaluative work. For example, the City of Westminster has a Family Recovery programme to assist persistent problem families. It costs around £19, 500 per family. Early estimates suggest that costs of just over £40,000 per family are avoided in the year which the family participates in the programme.[13]

17. The costs and benefits for any given policy are highly specific to the environment in which they are implemented. Demographics, labour market conditions and local infrastructure are but three examples of important contextual factors which can significantly change the costs and   benefits of programmes.

18. Recognising this has led pioneering areas such as Croydon, Birmingham and Manchester – to develop their own appraisal models – combining both high-quality research on the impact of their Early Intervention policies with relevant local data to allow better decisions on the most cost-effective mix of children's and young peoples services in their area.

19. Despite the difficulties in generalising cost-effectiveness from one area to another, the overarching message is that these programmes have positive returns. To spurn them risks adding new and substantial costs to society, as we demonstrate in the next section.

How much would it cost society to do nothing?

20. Some commentators have tried to quantify the total costs of inaction. For example, Action for Children and the New Economics Foundation have estimated that without their proposed additional early investment the economy could miss out of on returns of £486 billion over 20 years[14]. That is, £24 billion a year – equivalent to around one-fifth of projected health spending for 2010-11[15].

21. The examples below look in more detail at some of the costs associated with inaction:

• The productivity loss to the state as a result of youth unemployment is estimated at £10 million every day[16]. The average cost of an individual spending a lifetime on benefits is £430,000, not including or the loss of tax revenue[17].

- The cost of youth crime in 2009 alone has been estimated by the National Audit Office at between £8.5-£11 billion[18].

- The costs associated with mental health problems in the UK are estimated at 105.2 billion[19].

22. The total cost of drug misuse in the UK is estimated at £77.7 billion[20]. However as Sir Paul Ennals, chief executive of the National Children's Bureau, argues: "If you have a young man in drug rehabilitation it costs £250,000 a year, but the cost of family support that makes it less likely that he needs it costs only a fraction of that"[21].

23. The current total cost of children in care is estimated at £2.9 billion[22]. About half of this is spent on children who have been abused – dealing with a problem after it has become acute and costly rather than preventing it from happening.

24. Underpinning these aggregate costs are examples which show the costs associated with particular high-risk individuals, which can become much higher over time without effective intervention. Research from the London School of Economics[23] found that by the age of 28 the cumulative costs of public services were ten times higher for individuals with conduct disorder compared to those with no problems.

25. This is not a full and thorough cost-benefit analysis on the costs of inaction, but it gives a strong indication that there are many savings to be made.

26. We can ill afford to waste not only so much money, but also our children's prospects. This problem is not going to go away without action. And, as the following section illustrates, dysfunctional behaviour is, if anything, on the increase.

Why the problem won't go away without intervention

27. There is evidence that many of the problems Early Intervention seeks to address are worsening. For example, in England there is a strong upward trend in Special Educational Needs. The proportion of the school roll noted as having "without statement" – those who have special needs but have not been statemented – increased from 15.7 per cent in 2005 to 18.2 per cent in 2010[24].

28. Reviews of UK adolescent mental health have revealed worsening mental health problems amongst young people. Emotional problems, such as depression and anxiety, have been rising since the mid-1980s and conduct disorder has risen since the mid-1970s[25]. By comparison, the Netherlands and other countries did not experience such increases over the same periods.

29. The deteriorating state of adolescents' mental health would matter in any society at any time, but it matters more given our ageing population and the need for us to have an active workforce for the future.

Practical issues

Realising the benefits

30. There is another key point to be made about the potential benefits from Early Intervention programmes. One cannot achieve significant cost reductions on prisons or care homes simply by reducing the numbers in existing facilities. The real savings arise only through reducing the numbers to a point at which some prisons and care homes can be closed altogether. On current trajectories, our country will not be able to close any such facilities and instead will have to build more of them. Eliminating the need for such new facilities should be factored into the potential savings from Early Intervention.

31. A major additional complication is that successful Early Intervention programmes bring savings to many different agencies. Without pooled budgets, and agreement from those that save from Early Intervention that they will pay some of the cost, it becomes very difficult to win the economic case in some circles.

32. We hope that community budgets and the Early Intervention Grant will begin to address some of the issues concerning the need to pool and integrate different budgets which are aimed at alleviating the same problems or assisting the same individuals. However, Early Intervention programmes will not gather any momentum

unless the areas which pay for them realise savings from them. This means going further than community-based budgets. It entails ensuring that local areas and providers are incentivised by receiving a share of central government savings, for example on benefits or prisons. We return to this recommendation in chapter 5.

Moving to a better way to spend resources

33. A range of problems, described as "government and "market failures" by economists, such as (to use the somewhat inelegant phraseology) institutional fault-lines, perverse incentives, misaligned targets and poor data-sharing practices have historically blocked Early Intervention. In future, we must break down these barriers to attract decent investment and, in the case of data sharing, thereby enable the effective and early targeting of services. Localism and community budgets have an important role to play here, as discussed further in Chapter 5.

Success and failure

34. We need to use those programmes shown to be effective, innovate to create better ones and measure outcomes. Our ultimate test is whether our society can do for our social and emotional health what we have done for our physical health. The huge improvements in the physical health of children over the last century show us what is possible. Infant mortality has reduced 32-fold[26] and today's survival rates from most life-threatening childhood illnesses would have been unimaginable even 25 years ago.

35. However, the general good progress with respect to physical health and education has not been mirrored in children's mental health, including their behaviour and emotions. Rutter and Smith's[27] analysis of research and administrative data makes a compelling case for a decline in child mental health over the last century.

How do we know "What works"?

36. As expenditure on public sector services has grown there has been a growing interest in what is effective and ineffective. This can be a contentious area, with much dispute over what counts as reliable evidence. In recent years, however, there

has been a growing consensus in the scientific community about how to measure effectiveness reliably. Agreed standards have been taken up by health systems around the world, and by education, youth justice and social care systems in some parts of the world.

37. This review has adopted standards of evidence agreed by leading scientists in North America and Europe. These, rather than opinion or advocacy, have guided our view on 'what works'. The standards have been adopted by the Greater London Authority, with support from the Social Research Unit at Dartington. These standards (described in Appendix B) grade policies, programmes and practices on four dimensions as illustrated in the following box.

Standards of Evidence Dimensions

intervention specificity: is it clear who the programme is trying to help, by what means and with what intended effect?

evaluation quality: is the evaluation reliable, using methods such as random allocation to intervention and control groups, that will minimise bias and give a true indication about how much change can be attributed to the policy, programme or practice?

system ready: is the policy or practice ready to be taken to scale and delivered to the tens and hundreds of thousands of UK children that might benefit?

impact: using the single metric of the scale of the outcomes, how much change in the child's health and development can be attributed to the intervention?

---

38. As will be seen in Chapter 6, there are many programmes and policies that meet the standards of evidence adopted by this report. They are catalogued on 21 databases of effective intervention summarised in Appendix D. As will be seen, very few of these have been adopted in the UK.

39. Where they exist, several high-quality evaluations will be brought together in systematic reviews that give a sense of the range of effect

sizes of – or the possible outcomes which can be said to have resulted from – similar approaches across different settings. Such meta-analysis, to use the scientific term, is useful in that it gives an indication of the risks of a proven model not delivering the intended effects. Systematic reviews can thus increase the confidence in decisions made by purchasers and commissioners of public services.

Costs and benefits

40. As the quality of evaluation has improved over the last quarter century, so has the quality of cost-benefit analysis that translates the costs and impact of a policy or programme into a financial metric.

41. Several groups, both public and private, are working to improve the standards in this field. For example, the MacArthur Foundation has set up a centre at the University of Washington[28] in the United States that is aiming to set standards for cost-benefit analysis to improve the precision of estimates. The U.S. Institute of Medicine recently published a report on ways to better link cost-benefit analysis methods to effective public policy decision making[29]. In the UK, HM Treasury updates its Green Book[30], which provides guidance in this area for the public sector.

42. Think-tanks, and policy, research and academic institutes, such as the Washington State Institute for Public Policy, have developed models that can be adapted and used internationally for a variety of policy areas. The Social Research Unit at Dartington is translating the Washington model for use in the UK. Many of the estimates used in this Review come from this work.

What does success look like?

43. There is now a lot of confidence in the evidence about what does and does not work. But there is no silver bullet. As chapter 6 demonstrates, there are many routes to better outcomes for children supported by public services, even within the Early Intervention focus of this report.

44. For example, there is the potential to make small gains with lots of children. There is a class of proven Early Intervention programmes that operate in Sure Start Children's Centres and primary schools that improve children's social and emotional regulation. One class per week over two years produces children who are better able to moderate their emotional responses to, for example, relationships with other children and adults, or academic challenges in schools. The direct results are significant improvements in emotional well-being and behaviour. The indirect result is improvements in educational performance, because happier better behaved children learn more.

45. Another route to success is to seek big gains with a small, targeted high-risk group. The Family Nurse Partnership (FNP) is a proven Early Intervention model for children born to teenage mothers. It is one of the few illustrations of an evidence-based Early Intervention programme which is well delivered in the UK. It reaches over 6,000 families, a number that will more than double in the next four years. However, there is potential to expand further, and there are approximately 30,000 new families each year who could benefit from the programme.

46. 46. This report does not favour one approach over another. Our approach is to give local government and other purchasers of children's services reliable information about 'what works', when and how it does, and about the costs and benefits of evidence-based Early Intervention programmes. We hope, therefore, that scarce resources will be invested more wisely and lead to better outcomes for children.

47. However, to ensure that we are managing to improve outcomes for children, and making the most of the economic benefits of Early Intervention, we need better evaluation of existing programmes. We especially need an agreed and robust set of measures that determine the degree to which a child has the social and emotional bedrock needed to break the cycle of dysfunction. Such measures are suggested in the recent report of the Rt Hon Frank Field MP.[31] Meanwhile, the Tickell review of the Early Years Foundation Stage[32] is looking in more detail at the practicality of an early years development check at ages 24-36 months and/or the age of five, and Dame Clare Tickell will be making recommendations on this. Professor

Eileen Munro's review of child protection[33] is also looking at performance and data issues and is considering what measures, including those relating to Early Intervention, could and should be used to help drive continuously learning and adapting organisations. The next chapter will explore this issue, and make more specific and detailed recommendations to secure major improvements in Early Intervention provision.

RECOMMENDATIONS

48. Since waiting for problems to take root before reacting costs the taxpayer billions of pounds, I recommend that we should exploit the potential for massive savings in public expenditure through an Early Intervention approach.

Birmingham City Council started its Brighter Futures Programme in 2009. This transformational programme aims to measurably improve the physical health, behaviour and emotional health, literacy and numeracy, job skills and social literacy of Birmingham's children. It is described as a "system change for Early Intervention".

With an approach that brings together all partners it aims to develop, integrated children's services, focused on outcomes, which will:

- make the city a leader in investing resources to prevent problems emerging in children's lives;

- contain the increasing cost of services to children and young people which is occurring nationally due to rising demand;

- enable and support the expansion of integrated working practices across the city, develop leadership and increase the accuracy and currency of data.

The programme includes:

- **The development of systems and processes to support intelligent analysis of need** in order to inform the design of services, their commissioning, delivery and evaluation.

- **Improved service efficiency, integration and localisation**, both within the council and across partner agencies, allowing resources to shift towards preventative services and to support the implementation of improvements to services.

- **Mechanisms to support the cultural shift to services which are focused on prevention and Early Intervention**, while improving current services to children and young people with complex needs and continuing to deliver services within the council's corporate parenting and safeguarding responsibilities.

• **Identification of synergies with partners** and in particular the transition from children's to adult services.

Four pilot services for parents have been launched to-date. These have access to cost-effective prevention and Early Intervention programmes from pre-birth to adolescence that have an emphasis on targeted support for children in need. Programmes include the Family Nurse Partnership service for teenage parents.

All services and programmes are being independently evaluated, with a view to expanding them across the city, while bringing to an end services which fail to achieve the same, or sufficiently cost-effective, results.

Endnotes

1   Butterfield R, Henderson. J, Scott. R, Department of Health, Health Prevention and Expenditure in England: Health England Report 4, London 2009, piii, p13

2   Total place was an initiative that looked at how taking a whole area approach could lead to better services at less cost.

3   HM Treasury and Department for Communities and Local Government, Total Place: a whole area approach to public services, 2010, p17

4   Hussey, R. (2010). *Measurement Investment in Prevention.* North West Strategic Heatlh Authority, Manchester

5   NHS Croydon & Croydon Council, Child: Family: Place: *Radical efficiency to improve the outcomes of young children,* 2010, p33

6   Organisation for Economic Cooperation and Development, Doing Better for Children, 2009,

7   Allen G and Duncan Smith I, "Early Intervention: Good Parents, Great Kids, Better Citizens" London 2008

8   Karoly, LA., Rebecca, K, Cannon J.S. 2005 Early Childhood Interventions: proven results, Future Promise. Santa Monica, Calif. RAND Corporation.

9   S.Aos, R. Lieb, J. Mayfield, M. Miller, & A. Pennucci. Benefits and costs of prevention and Early Intervention programs for youth, 2004 Olympia: Washington State Institute for Public Policy, Document No. 04-07-3901,

10   Lynch. R, "Early Childhood Investment yields big Payoff, WestEd, 2005

11   C4EO, "Grasping the Nettle: Early Intervention for children, families and communities, 2010, p27

12   The Literacy Hour, Machin, S, McNally. S, 2007, Journal of Public Economics 92, p1441-1462

13   City of Westminster, Repairing broken families and rescuing fractured communities: lessons from the frontline.

14   Backing the Future: why investing in children is good for us all. Action for Children and New Economics Foundation report, September 2009.

15   HM Treasury, Budget 2010, p5

16   The Cost of Exclusion: Counting the cost of youth disadvantage in the UK, Princess Trust,

17   Allen G and Duncan Smith I "Early Intervention: Good Parents, Great Kids, Better Citizens" 2008, p33

18   Report by the Comptroller and Auditor General, National Audit Office, The youth justice system in England and Wales: Reducing offending by young people, 2010, p4

19   The Economic and Social Costs of Mental Health

Problems in 2009/10. Centre for Mental Health

20 Backing the future: Why investing in children is good for us all,

21 Speaking at the launch of 'Early Intervention City', in Nottingham.

22 Department for Education, Outturn data archive, Outturn summary 2009-10, 2011, Available at: http://www.education.gov.uk/childrenandyoungpeople/strategy/financeandfunding/section251/archive/a0071834/outturn-data-archive

23 Scott. S, Knapp. M, Henderson. J, Maughan, B, Financial cost of social exclusion: follow up study of antisocial children into adulthood, British Medical Journal, 2001, Vol 323, p1-5

24 Department for Education, Special Education Needs in England, January 2010 Statistical First Release

25 The Nuffield Foundation, Time Trends in adolescent mental well-being, 2004 Seminar on Children and Families.

26 NEED A REFERENCE OUTSTANDING

27 Rutter M and Smith DJ, Towards causal explanations of time trends in psychosocial disorders of youth. In M Rutter and DJ Smith (eds) *Psychosocial disorders in young people: Time trends and their causes*. Chichester: Wiley, 1995

28 Macarthur foundation, 2011, Available at: http://www.macfound.org/site/c.lkLXJ8MQKrH/b.947545/k.D8C1/Domestic_Grantmaking__Policy_Research__Recent_Grants.htm

29 Benefit-Cost Analysis for Early Childhood Interventions. Workshop Summary, 2009, Available at: http://www.iom.edu/Reports/2009/Benefit-Cost-Analysis-for-Early-Childhood-Interventions.aspx

30 HM Treasury, Green Book, 2003, Available at: http://www.hm-treasury.gov.uk/data_greenbook_index.htm

31 The Foundation years: preventing poor children becoming poor adults, the report of the Independent Review on Poverty and Life Chances, Frank Field, December 2010

32 The forthcoming review of the Early Years Foundation Stage curriculum by Dame Clare Tickell"

33 Munro Review of Child Protection at http://www.education.gov.uk/munroreview/firstreport.shtml

Part 2:
The Way Forward

Introduction to Part 2

1. Part 1 of the report revealed that there are still too many children with inadequate social and emotional capabilities, and that this affects how they develop through all the stages of their lives, including mental well-being, education, employment and family. Such problems are not confined only to individuals and their families: they may have devastating effects on the wider society in terms of crime and social disruption and fragmentation generally. There are additional costs in childhood for health, education, social work and criminal justice agencies. In the adult life, the number of productive workers available to hard-pressed employers is reduced, dependency on the state is generated and there is only a life of misery for those most affected. It is evident that impairments concentrate (but not wholly) in poor families, and handicap most those children born into families whose parents themselves lacked a social and emotional bedrock.

2. The Review shows that despite important policies such as Sure Start children's centres, major investments in last decade have not paid the expected dividends in terms of children's well-being. My analysis revealed that the importance of the early years, especially for those afflicted by inter-generational deprivation, is still not fully appreciated. Public sector investments tend to be skewed to a time when it is too late to have much hope of success.

3. The Review came across many examples of high quality Early Intervention that worked throughout childhood. Early Intervention reaps the greatest benefit in the first years of life, but there are also opportunities to help create the excellent parents of future generations by continuing to build a social and emotional bedrock from the ages of 0-18 and by responding to, say, the first signs of reading difficulty in primary school, or the first glimmer of anti-social behaviour in secondary school or the first indications of relationship problems in early adulthood.

4. My analysis has left me in no doubt of the economic benefits associated with high-quality Early Intervention. Moreover, at a time of great strain on public finances, there is good reason to believe that private as well as public investors can see the economic possibilities represented by Early Intervention, and the second report of my Review in the first half of 2011 will explore how these opportunities can be realised.

5. In Part Two of this report I now turn to examine how a number of pre-existing efforts by government can be transformed by taking them one step further, not by boundless resources or Statutory dictat – which has not exactly done the trick in recent decades.Instead I suggest using well worn practises-an effective plan, synthesis not silo, freeing up local talent, training and motivating your workforce, expanding what works, accurately assessing progress in order to assist it and bringing in allies to crusade for a cause.

6. I cannot claim that my Review has uncovered new ground. Much of what has been said here has been said before. So why have we not responded accordingly? In the last chapter of Part I set out some of the obstacles that stand in the way of implementation of effective Early Intervention policies and practices.

7. This analysis has led me to the following conclusions, which I set out more fully in the second part of the Review. We need more Early Intervention to pre-empt problems or to respond to the first signs of risk to healthy child development. Our goal should be for society – families, communities, public, I voluntary and private sector agencies – to provide children with the social and emotional foundations needed for a productive life. Although intervention is cheaper and more effective when done at the earliest opportunity, we can also help the next generation by assisting the social and emotional development of future parents, threats throughout life, from conception to birth, from birth to primary school, during the secondary school years, and into early adulthood.

8. I have concluded that there are much greater opportunities to intervene early to help children to be ready for school (for primary school), ready for work (as they leave secondary school or university) and ready for life (to be loving and nurturing parents themselves).I have concluded that any additional investment should be concentrated on Early Intervention in the early years and on Early Intervention at all prior stages of child development – before birth, before primary school, before secondary school and before to higher education and work.

9. As in all aspects of life, the quality of Early Intervention matters. For that reason I am promoting evidence-based Early Intervention, such as that represented in a series of Early Intervention programmes described in the following chapter.

10. It is also plain to me that communities and local agencies cannot rely on one type of Early Intervention. A combination of approaches that are financially sustainable is needed. I am, therefore recommending, in Chapter 7 that there is a focus of Early Intervention in places that will demonstrate what can be achieved. In the second part of my Review I will set out how these places can be supported with new kinds of funding.

11. However, in conclusion, I strongly believe that neither my Review nor government can tell those leading the expansion of Early Intervention activity what to do. Central direction has been tried and found wanting. I want to support local people to make local decisions based on the best independent investment, policy, practice and other advice from a new Early Intervention Foundation, as described in Chapter Eight.

12. But first, what can we do better that we do now?

Chapter 5
Moving on

If we are to give every child the chance to live a happy and successful life we need to act while they are in the early years. Dealing with the problems of educational failure, family breakdown and other symptoms of the broken society is a priority for a future Conservative Government

Rt Hon David Cameron MP, 2008

Early intervention programmes with a proven impact will be promoted. Our radical Total Place agenda will take this further, giving local areas additional freedom to achieve better services and more savings, cutting bureaucracy and management costs, while placing a greater on early intervention.

Labour Party manifesto, April 2010

We will improve discipline by early intervention to tackle the poor basic education of those children who are otherwise most likely to misbehave and become demotivated.

Liberal Democrat Party manifesto, April 2010

Introduction

1. All parties have committed to give priority to early intervention, as the quotations above testify and in this report so far I have demonstrated why Early Intervention is important for people and good for the economy and deserves the support of those of all parties and none... In this chapter I look at how existing policies, briefly reviewed in chapter 3, can be taken further as and when resources permit, and be given the political and administrative encouragement they need. I then examine some of the obstacles to implementing the key recommendations of chapters 6 to 8 of this report.

2. As I have already shown, recent governments have taken some excellent preliminary action on Early Intervention. My intention in this section is to see if these can be taken **a little** further **to fundamentally reshape provision in the direction of Early Intervention** and to come up with a practical set of recommendations which recognise the current public expenditure constraints and make reference to the work of other current reviews of major social issues.

The foundation years

3. To shift policy to earlier intervention and prevention we need to ensure wider recognition that pregnancy and the first few years are essential to building a good foundation for life, reducing inequalities and promoting social mobility. It is for this reason that I support the recommendation in the Independent Review on Poverty and Life Chances, by Rt Hon Frank Field MP, that local and national government should give greater identity to the "foundation years", that is that period from pregnancy to the age of five.[1]

Recommendation

4. I recommend that the United Kingdom should adopt the concept of the *Foundation Years stage, from 0-5* (including pregnancy), and give it at least the same status and recognition as primary or secondary stages. Its prime objective should be to produce high levels of *"school readiness"* for all children regardless of family income. To support this recommendation, I further recommend that all year groups should be numbered from birth, not from the start of primary school. This will help everyone with responsibilities for child development, particularly parents, to understand how the 0-18 health and educational cycle is continuous from birth and does not start on entry to primary school.

Greater local financial freedom

Building on the Early Intervention Grant and Community Budgets

5. To achieve real change local areas will need to work together – formally or informally – to endorse, plan and fund an organisational and cultural shift towards Early Intervention from all those engaged in local service provision. The contribution of parents and carers and the voluntary and community sector is also very important. This must match and support the change in national priorities **toward Early Intervention.**

6. The government has recently announced the creation of Community Budget areas, where budgets from a range of relevant sources (including the Early Integration Grant) will be able to be pooled to create a single budget to provide integrated services for families with multiple problems We welcome this development and have been keeping in touch with its progress. It was intended largely to address the needs of exactly those families who would benefit from early intervention. As chapter 7 will illustrate, a number of Community Budget areas have also agreed to be Early Intervention places. This is an excellent start.

7. However, this measure alone will not solve the major issues that we have addressed in chapters 1 and 2, although the Early Intervention Grant does provide an incredibly powerful symbol. However, in these times of financial constraint **the Community Budget** will be subject to many demands. I hope chapters 6,7 and 8 in particular can inform decisions around the use of the Early Intervention Grant in those areas with Community Budgets on how best to spend limited resources, and help directors of services make a case for reallocating spending away from historical allocations. We would hope that the government would back us on this aim.

8. The government has also made money available for disadvantaged children in school through the pupil premium and the Education Endowment Funds. We believe that this money should be spent on activities and programmes that are shown to be cost-effective in improving children's lives and tackling inequalities, and that is exactly what the programmes identified in chapter 6 in this report will achieve.

9. The Department for Communities and Local Government need to continue examine how to develop with local authorities the incentives to provide effective, connected early intervention services. Their benefits accrue to many agencies, some of them national. Therefore, we need to ensure that we reward local authorities whose early intervention strategies result in lower costs to national government so that they can continue to invest in this area. This entails effectively tracking the success of programmes and providing payment by results where appropriate

10. Going with the grain of current government policy, I believe that central government needs to provide local government with more freedom and flexibility to use its income, whether locally

generated or received from central government, in order that Early Intervention can develop in the best interests of children and young people in their communities. .

11. The introduction of the Early Intervention Grant, alongside the proposals in the Public Health White Paper,[2] the Munro review and the introduction of Community Budgets, gives local areas a real opportunity to increase the effectiveness (including cost-effectiveness), connection and integration of services for children and families. But these are only small steps in a long journey to greater local freedom. This is relevant to the wide range of services that provide support to these children and families. **These include maternity and community child and health services (such as health visitors, midwives), GPs, children's social care, and parenting**. This would achieve successful outcomes in education (including early years education) and achieve successful transitions through the education system.

12. In line with these developments, my second report will make proposals on how the Treasury, working with central government departments and local authority finance professionals, can devise a way in which the future savings that arise from Early Intervention can be used to increase investment in Early Intervention services . I accept that this will require considerable ingenuity and imagination, because the savings in future expenditure from Early Intervention will accrue to many different areas or agencies and not necessarily the one making the initial investment. But the same thing can be said of many other capital investments which are routinely made in the public sector. For example, when a local authority invests in a major road improvement scheme, it provides benefits to traffic from other areas and (by reducing stress and accidents) it reduces future expenditures for the police and the NHS. I strongly believe that the returns from Early Intervention, even on conservative estimates, will be big enough and clear enough to provide a more-than-adequate return on the initial investment required, if the way can be found to release them. An independent Early Intervention Foundation, which I recommend below, could ultimately take a new look at local and central government

financial processes, and provide robust estimates of the expected accruals to different bodies from particular Early Intervention systems and programmes, and independent monitoring of programme effectiveness.

13. It was obvious from the visits of the Review team and from all the evidence received that the devolved settlement has had a profoundly stimulating and creative impact on Early Intervention work in Northern Ireland, Wales and Scotland which I would hope to see replicated in a more empowered English local government.

14. However having spoken at length to many local councils during the period of this Review, their biggest fear is that the new freedoms granted by central government could just as easily be taken away from them should government change its mind or its political complexion. This would be a serious blow to Early Intervention, which depends on sustainability and taking a long term view **after all, Early Intervention affects generations yet unborn**. I would, therefore, hope that there could be some stability in the settlement of powers between local and central government. Perhaps the best way forward would be for the settlement to be agreed between the two and given some authority as a code with some statutory safeguards. There could be many other advantages from such a settlement, but my report must be limited to Early Intervention.

Recommendation

15. Since a successful Early Intervention approach requires sustainability and a long-term view, I recommend that the Secretary of State for Communities and Local Government creates a lasting, stable settlement between central and local government within *a published framework or codification of the local/central relationship*. I further recommend that this settlement be agreed by all political parties, and adhered to whichever of them are in power in central or local government.

16. My second report on the use and sources of alternative funding mechanisms will provide further recommendations in the area of the financial relationship of the centre and the localities.

Making the most of changes to the health services

17. The upheaval in local health services may present opportunities for health to play an even more important role in Early Intervention than it does now. It should also be the cue for much more integrated working between health and education at national level where it was apparent even in drafting my report that there was room for improvement. The transitions between health and education are not always immediately clear and whatever ministerial co-ordination proposals for Early Intervention are adopted (see chapter 9, this must be one of the first areas to be addressed. If the 0-5 foundation years are to become a reality a plan of action with widespread support and dissemination has to be agreed between the education and health departments.It should set out the vision for vthe 0-5's,the problems and how to address them,the curriculum for the 0-5's,and possiblythe greatest challenge of all-it should be readable by constituents on my council estates and by MP's.Finally it should be presented jointly by the Secretaries of State for scrutiny by the House Select Committees and then formally endorsed by Parliament and subject to an Annual progress report to Parliament.

Recommendation

18. I recommend that the Department of Health and the Department for Education work together with other partners and interests to produce within 18 months one seamless *Foundation Years Plan* from pregnancy to 5 years of age: this Plan should be widely understood and disseminated in order to make the 0-5 Foundation years a reality. I recommend that this Plan is endorsed by Parliament.

Local health

19. For many children up to the age of three, contact with health professionals will be their only contact with officials.The local health service can make a real difference.Health services, working with partners, have a critical role to play in early intervention, especially during pregnancy up to when a child is five years of age, when families and children need clinical as well as psycho-social

and educational interventions and support from health and early years professionals. However, the change in the numbers of health visitors, variations in coverage of the Healthy Child Programme and variation in the levels of provision of ante-natal education and preparation for parenthood suggest that there is more that can be done to ensure there is universal provision in pregnancy and early childhood.

20. Pregnancy and the post-natal period are key times for early interventions. It is when expectant mothers are motivated to learn and want to do the best for their child. In the 2010 survey of women's experiences of maternity services, the Care Quality Commission found that 38 per cent of women reported not being offered any ante-natal classes.[3] Health and early years services need to do more to ensure that expectant mother and fathers are offered high-quality community-based preparation for parenthood that includes learning about the needs of babies during pregnancy and early life and how to make the successful transition to parenthood.

21. The Healthy Child Programme is the universal public health programme providing regular health and development reviews, screening tests, immunisations, health promotion and parenting support from pregnancy to 19 years of age. In the important first years of life the HCP is led and provided by health visiting teams, ensuring that all children and families receive support from health professionals as well as more targeted support for those who need it through universal and specialist services. The expansion of the number of health visitors is key because for many families in the early years of life the health visitor is their main contact with children's services. I encourage the health system to develop strong universal public health through to increase the focus of pregnancy and early years on disadvantaged families, as outlined in *Healthy Lives, Healthy People* (2010)[4].

22. The priority should be to equip health visitors, those established and those to be recruited, and their teams, with an understanding of early childhood development and proven ways of working with families on the promotion of strong social and emotional capability in children.

23. I welcome the government's commitment to recruit 4,200 new health visitors by 2015 and to double capacity of the Family Nurse Partnership programme. The expansion of the health visiting service, supported by the FNP, will mean increased capacity to support mothers and families where mental health issues may have a detrimental impact on the child. I hope that the new mental health strategy will reflect the need to further support maternal mental health.

24. Health professionals (GPs, midwives and health visitors) play a key role in supporting child development and in referring mothers and children who might need additional help to more targeted support.

25. I suggest that this is done by ensuring that there are clear public health outcomes for children in the early years related to the Healthy Child Programme and health visiting as well as FNP. As the arrangements proposed in the Public Health White Paper[5] develop, health and wellbeing boards and directors of public health will be well placed to focus on children's public health outcomes and promote strong contributions from all local partners, both within the health field and from other organisations working to achieve the same outcomes.

26. Under the new organisational arrangements for health it is important that the focus on ante-natal education and preparation for parenthood, health visiting and FNP is not lost in the redistribution of functions that always accompanies such an upheaval. GP consortia and local authorities work together to commission evidence-based preventative early interventions, especially in pregnancy and the first years of life.

27. The new health and well-being boards will allow local authorities to take a strategic approach to promote integration of health, adult social care and children's services. They could be an appropriate body to lead integrated Early Intervention strategies at local level.

28. The Department of Health and NHS should also further strengthen the leadership role of directors of public health for improving early childhood development as the arrangements set out in the Public Health White Paper develop.[6]

Measures should include a review at two to 2½ years to look at development and health and readiness for school. Progress here should inform the joint strategic needs assessments. These will be drawn up by GP consortia, local authorities, police forces and other organisations under the arrangements for the new health and well-being boards, they should include improving the social and emotional capability of children, Directors of public health will have a key role in ensuring that these assessments support the health and well-being boards to promote a new high- level consensus on local priorities for early childhood development between consortia, local authorities, their elected members and other key partners. This should lead to agreed actions and future joint working through the proposed Joint Health and Wellbeing Strategy.[7]

Recommendations

29. I believe that under the government's proposed *new arrangements for local health* services, a great opportunity exists to localise Early Intervention and I recommend that one of the reorganisation's key themes should be a focus on antenatal education/preparation for parenthood, social and emotional development for the under 3's. I recommend

- that *GP consortia* and local authorities work together to commission evidence-based preventative Early Interventions, especially in pregnancy and the first years of life.

- that the proposed new local *'Health and Wellbeing Boards'* should create integrated Early Intervention strategies based on Joint Strategic Needs Analysis at local level, share best practice and have the freedom to tie into the institutional arrangements for Early Intervention recommended below;

- that the Department of Health and the NHS further strengthen the accountability of *local Directors of Public Health* for improving social and emotional capability.

Better parental leave arrangements

30. It may be that the earlier the intervention the more effective and long lasting it can be, but public

spending does not reflect this truism, as spending is focused higher up the spectrum of need, once problems have already escalated. Intervention is then more costly. The earlier the intervention the less need for more intensive and more expensive interventions later, and costs that accrue to the welfare and criminal justice systems. This imbalance must be redressed.

31. The quality of a child's relationships and learning experiences in the family has more influence on future achievement than innate ability, material circumstances or the quality of pre-school and school provision. Therefore, parents need to have time for those positive experiences with their children, and this means that we need to consider a move to a more generous and flexible maternity and paternity benefit system, and flexible working practices.

32. Currently in the UK all female employees are entitled to 52 weeks of maternity leave. In the first six weeks women are entitled to 90 per cent of their pay. However, after that many are paid only the statutory minimum of £124.88 per week for the remaining 39 weeks of paid leave Of course, some employers are more generous, but the fact is that many women cannot afford to take the full year off work, and the average length of maternity leave is only six months.[8]

33. In Sweden working parents are entitled to share 16 months of parental leave and at least two months need to be taken by the minority parent, – **the one taking the least of the 16 months** (usually the father) to encourage his or her involvement in child rearing. The first 390 days are paid at approximately 80 per cent of previous income. There is also the flexibility to go back to work part-time, and top up income with the benefit. The cost is shared between the employer and the state.

34. It is clear that moving towards a more generous system would be unacceptably expensive at the moment. However, given the exceptional and lasting importance of the first period of any child's life, and the huge savings resulting from getting this right, I am convinced that parental leave arrangements should be a top priority for the redistribution of existing spending or new public expenditure in more favourable times. I

suggest that serious consideration is given to the proposals, to be consulted on this spring in n inter-departmental government consultation paper, for a system of flexible parental leave which enables parents to take more of their entitlement. However, thinking further ahead, I recommend the formation of a broad-based all-party review to examine options and cost benefits to move the UK towards Swedish standards of parental leave, as resources allow, within a realistic timescale.

Recommendations

35. I recommend the formation of a broad based all-party group to explore possible means of giving British parents and babies similar benefits in *maternity and paternity support* to those now enjoyed by their Swedish counterparts and their babies.

Expansion of Family Nurse Partnerships

36. In the US the Nurse Family Partnership is the example which Early Intervention models are judged by. It benefits those children born to first time mothers with low psychological resources, in particular teenage mothers living in poverty. The programme has 30 years of evidence to back it up in the USA and has been implemented successfully in England over the last four years, where it is called the Family Nurse Partnership programme. FNP is a preventive programme of structured home visiting for young first time mothers, provided by specially trained nurses, from early pregnancy until their child is two years of age. FNP offers high-intensity support through home visits using methods to build self-efficacy and promote attachment and positive parenting with practical activities that change behaviour and tackle the emotional problems that prevent some mothers and fathers caring well for their child. It has been particularly successful in connecting with those most disaffected with and distrustful of services.

37. The potential benefits of this programme could be reaped by agencies responsible for health (better antenatal health, mental health and fewer hospital attendances) safeguarding (prevention of child maltreatment), youth justice (less offending) and education (better school performance and less school dropout). There are also gains for the

Department of Work and Pensions (more parents in work) and the Ministry of Justice (reduced demand on court, prison and probation services).

38. Evidence from the USA:

- Savings of between $17,000 and $34,000 per child by the time they reach the age of 15, **or** $3-$5 for every $1 invested, **with greatest gains for greatest for** high risk groups.[9]

- The costs of programme are recovered by the time children aged four due to reduced health service use and reduced welfare use and increased earnings of mother (in Elmira trial Savings increase as children get older.

- Identified as the most cost-effective child welfare and home visiting programme in a study by Washington State Institute for Public Policy.

- The largest cost savings are due to reductions in welfare use (mother), increased earnings and increased tax revenue (mother) and less involvement with criminal justice (mother and child)

- Recently published US evidence suggests that NFP saves the government substantial amounts in welfare payments alone with $12,300 saved for each family from the time when the child is born to its reaching 12 years old.(Early findings from the formative evaluation in England are encouraging[10] but it is too early to know what the impact and cost benefits of the FNP are in this country compared with universal services. For this reason a large scale trial to evaluate FNP in England is being undertaken.)

- Estimates about the sums saved are conservative as they do not include all the benefits.

39. It is a tribute to the programme that even in a time of public expenditure constraint the government recently announced plans to double the number of places so that over 13, 000 families can benefit at any one time by 2015. In the longer term FNP could be established as a core Early Intervention programme for vulnerable first time young mothers in this country alongside universal health visiting and other Early Intervention programmes. This will rely on the evaluation of the programme impacts through the research trial and overcoming barriers to an explanation

and ensuring sustainability and momentum in the next four years. I welcome the government's commitment to measured expansion and making sure that this is achieved through the Operating Framework

40. The Family Nurse Partnership is one of the strongest and most innovative programmes around. If FNP is found to be cost effective our aspiration should be to offer it to all vulnerable first time young mothers as it could produce quantifiable social and economic benefits from increased investment

41. The allocations to primary care trusts for 11/12 provide them with £89 billion to spend on the local frontline services, including FNP, an increase of £2.6 billion, or three per cent.

42. In the longer term funding for expansion of FNP could come from other sources as well as the public purse and be assisted by the institutional arrangements outlined in chapters 6,7,and 8,and the deployment of the new financial instruments which I expect to propose in my second report this summer. If my key recommendations are accepted, I propose that the Early Intervention Foundation would open up preliminary discussions with the Family Nurse Partnership National Unit of the Department of Health about how a pragmatic expansion could take place and how non-government investment could be attracted to the venture.

43. Finally, FNP does not exist in isolation but exists within universal early intervention and prevention services supporting health visitors and Sure Start children's centres. These wider services and the professionals who work in them can learn from FNP in particular how it engages marginalised groups, effects behaviour change and offers a model of supervision. It is important that the FNP National Unit works with local FNP sites to explore opportunities to share the learning with health visitors and the centres.

Recommendation

44. I recommend that the success of *Family Nurse Partnership* should be taken further, with the specific aspiration subject to the on-going DH evaluation, that every vulnerable first time

young mother who meets the criteria and wants Family Nurse Partnership should be able to access it and that discussions should take place with all relevant interests on how to ensure sustained local commissioning, leadership and finance. I anticipate that this would be one of the first programmes to be funded through one of the additional funding mechanisms now under consideration which will be outlined in my second Report.

Making the most of Sure Start children's centres

45. The development of children's centres, aimed at children under five and their families has enabled integrated services to be developed in new and innovative ways, flexibly and in response to local need. The integrated working between professionals, which the centres have encouraged, particularly by midwives and health visitors, can enable vulnerable families to start to make use of services they otherwise find hard to reach. Although children's centres are a relatively recent concept, many are already successfully using evidence based programmes (for example, Triple P and Webster Stratton Incredible Years).[11] The government's focus on increasing the use of programmes, based on evidence, in children's centres, and paying providers, in part, by the results they achieve, should help ensure that more families are supported by services which have proven their effectiveness.

46. It is encouraging to note the government's recent statement that there is enough money in the Early Intervention Grant to maintain the existing network of children's centres.[12]

47. I believe that centres should be in a strong position to provide an environment centred on children and families, where services of proven worth, such as those described in chapter 6, that best meet their needs, can be joined together on their behalf. Health services are key to centres in engaging vulnerable families as well as offering the full range of Early Intervention services

48. Local areas will be best placed to understand the most appropriate model that ensures parents, children and young people can have the services they require. This must include provision that reaches to those parents, children and

young people and families in the greatest need, particularly those who have no current access to what they need.

49. Greater freedom and less central prescription is a real opportunity for local authorities to think long-term and focus on what works. The Community Budget programme is a good first step to achieving this.

Recommendations

50. I recommend that future expansion of Early Intervention programmes should favour those which combine strong evidence bases with impact on crucial stages in the development of social and emotional bedrock in children, and that the present national network of Children's Centres should use such approaches, including evidence-based evaluation systems, to identify and meet the needs of vulnerable children and families. This could include programmes such as FNP. I support the proposal in the Schools White Paper that the forthcoming National College of School Leadership should provide training for Children's Centre leaders, and recommend that this should include training on social and emotional development and evidence-based Early Intervention approaches.

51. I recommend that the proposal in the schools White Paper[13], that the National College of School Leadership should provide training for children's centre leaders on social and emotional development and evidence-based approaches.

Assessing social and emotional progress

Assessing social and emotional progress

52. Of all the many important recommendations in this report, this one ,along with the one on an Early Intervention Foundation are the most important to me.

53. Just as we can barely believe that tiny children were sent up chimneys, I believe in years to come future generations will be aghast that we let children enter school when they were not school ready, and subjected them to 11 or more humiliating and underachieving years – which then cost the taxpayer billions to pick up the broken pieces. Now we have a much cheaper and more

effective alternative, to intervene early to provide children and families with the support they need to overcome barriers and succeed in life. To do that Health and Education-who do so much excellent work separately – must work much more closely together on the assessment of 0 to 5 year olds and have a single strategy for it.

54. The Department for Education has a strong evidence base for its focus on introducing new support for the early years by retaining a universal offer, while also ensuring that services and opportunities reach those in greatest need[14, 15]. The new entitlement for disadvantaged [those from the bottom 20% of earners] 2-year-olds to 15 hours of free early education a week should be a tremendous boost to help children develop their social and emotional capability especially if it is not happening at home. This is likely to improve take-up of nursery education at age 3 – and therefore educational attainment at school. Many authorities who took part in the pilot scheme felt that joining up this offer with services for family support and health was particularly valuable in improving wider outcomes for families. However the key questions here are the learning and development support for young children and the workforce. Warehousing young children with low quality early years provision will be a criminal waste of this unrepeatable opportunity to help the 2 year olds who would benefit most. We discuss the workforce later, however it is vital that the support young children receive for their learning and development helps build the social and emotional bedrock of this age group.

55. Ensuring that as many children as possible meet key milestones in the early years is the central purpose of intervention in the early years.

56. It is possible to wait until just before school begins and have a booster programme, however a far better approach is to help children achieve milestones as they grow, giving a little extra help as it is needed rather than just before school. Therefore regular and effective assessment of the 0-5's is crucial Assessment to gauge attainment and school readiness earlier, and identify and provide support to those not school-ready, is needed.

Identifying those who need help.

57. Universal services provided by GPs, hospitals, midwives, health visiting teams, Children's Centres, nurseries, schools, housing and police can have all been shown to be effective in raising standards of physical health and/or educational attainment. However, they should now be more clearly charged with responsibility for improving standards of social and emotional well-being, and to recognise specifically the importance of the early years. In short, these agencies should all be working together to make sure that a child is school ready.

58. We need to use the evidence based universal Healthy Child Programme schedule of health and development checks from pregnancy onwards more effectively. Led by health visitors in collaboration with SSCCs and General Practice, the HCP should identify those children and families needing additional input to be school ready. All the responsible agencies should all work towards improving school readiness, and where they cannot achieve this, they should swiftly refer those needing particular help to appropriate specialised services.

59. Local authorities with their health partners also have a key role to play in promoting and brokering integrated working at a local level and in ensuring there is open access to universal services and that children and families at risk who may not present themselves through universal services are identified.

Local data

60. To ease identification and targeting we strongly support the recent recommendation[16] by Rt Hon Frank Field MP that local authorities should be able to pool data and track the children most in need in their areas. The life chances of our children and indeed their children should not be sacrificed by the 'computer says no' mentality that so often hinders local data sharing. For this to work the government should review legislation that prevents local authorities, and others such as the police, using existing data to identify and support families who are most in need. It should make it easier for local authorities to use data for this purpose and provide a template for successful data -sharing which respects data privacy issues. This has been

a source of local frustration for many many years.In order to bring this question to a hrad I recommend that after thorough preparation local and central government meet to bottom out this problem,sweep away yhe excuses and mythology and seek to put data tracking on a more certain and rational footing so that our children can benefit from the earliest intervention appropriate.

61. It would also be useful to keep track of actual success or failure to prepare children to be life ready and child ready. If we truly seek to break intergenerational cycles of dysfunction we must know the number of children whose life chances are being improved by early intervention policies. Such measures will also inform future policy making regarding the efficacy of early intervention programmes

Recommendation I recommend that a meeting between the Local Government Association and departmental ministers is convened to iron out problems around *data sharing* at local level.

62. This report supports the recommendations made by Rt Hon Frank Field MP[17] for his set of national Life Chances Indicators. These were:.

- Cognitive development at age 3 – language and communication development, problem solving skills and school readiness – suggested measures are the British Ability Scales (in particular the naming vocabulary and picture similarities sub-scales) and Bracken School Readiness Assessment;

- Behavioural, social and emotional development at age three – Emotional health, behavioural and conduct problems, hyperactivity, peer relationships and positive behaviour – suggested measures are Strengths and Difficulties Questionnaire for three to four year olds

- Physical development at age three – Body mass index (BMI) and general health of child – suggested measures are Height and weight to calculate BMI and Parental rating of child's general health.

63. I believe that these checks must be carried out before the first year of school and that they should form one part of an integrated health and education assessment linked to the Healthy Child

Programme health and development review at two to two and a half years.

64. We have made the strongest representations on this to the forthcoming review of the Early Years Foundation Stage curriculum by Dame Clare Tickell and would support any of her proposals which ensures that support for young children's learning and development and development checks for this age group foster the development of social and emotional capability and ensures a child's readiness for school. The Tickell review is looking in more detail at the assessment of young children, and will be making recommendations on this. There is a wonderful opportunity here to link the assessment carried out by early years practitioners to those of the health visitor's two to two and a half years review which is part of the Healthy Child programme.This will avoid duplication and waste of resources and result in a seamless set of regular assessments covering the social and emotional development of all 0-5 year olds.

65. I also welcome the commitment in the Department of Health's Healthy Lives, Healthy People: Transparency in Outcomes consultation, to reflect the findings of the Frank Field Review in the Public Health Outcomes Framework, where appropriate. The Public Health Outcomes Framework[18] will provide a context for public health activity across the whole of the public health system. The current plan is that it will include a set of indicators based on nationally collated and analysed data relating to public health (thereby minimising the burden on local authorities). The consultation closes on 31 March 2011.

66. So in conclusion while I strongly recommend the universal implementation of the Healthy Child Programme schedule of health and developmental reviews including assessment of social skills and emotional development, attachment and wider family relationships at 2 to2.5 years. It is not enough. The HCP should be linked more closely to the Early Years Foundation Stage, with its valuable emphasis on assessing a child's readiness for school. This more integrated programme of reviews for all children should explore the opportunities for national measures based on those being developed by Frank Field and the Department of Health, and local assessment as being delivered through

the health visitor 2 – 2.5 year old review, and the opportunities for joining this up with the early years assessment as being explored by Dame Clare Tickell as part of her review. . The Department for Education and Department for Health should work together, with local authorities and health services, to test the feasibility of such measures and early assessment.

Recommendation.

67. I recommend that every child has *a clear schedule of social and emotional reviews up to and including the age of 5* so that they can be put on the path to "school readiness "which many -not least from low income households- would benefit from. Accountability is confused and divided, policy is incomplete and there is an unnecessary separation between the Healthy Child Programme reviews and the Early Years Foundation stage assessments. It is timely that several external reviews are taking place. Providing they result in a regular and coherent series of assessments Government should act swiftly to ensure that the 0 to 5's are helped at the earliest and most cost effective point in their lives to develop the social and emotional bedrock upon which they can thrive.

The quality of the workforce

68. Children's centres and other early years settings have already worked hard to provide more user-friendly and integrated services that reach disadvantaged communities with no ready access to the services they need. My Review team has seen examples of children's centres already engaging with evidence-based programmes (for example, Family Nurse Partnership, Healthy Child Programme, and structured parenting programmes). Some more established children's centres are increasingly focusing on well-evidence approaches as well, taking a "practitioner researcher" approach, where staff continually reflect on the impact of their work

69. However, I am not confident that every children's centre is doing this yet. Similarly, significant work has been carried out by the Children's Workforce Development Council to develop the early years' workforce.

70. Workforce development will remain critical – in early education for example, evidence clearly shows that quality matters to child outcomes and narrowing the gap in learning and development[19]. Children's centre leaders and staff (particularly those working in early education and in outreach and family support) need to be well qualified and well supervised, and to have opportunities to develop skills which enable them to use evidence-based approaches. The UK *EPPE* study[20] has shown the strong relationship between the of the quality of early childcare and outcomes, and all this especially more so for disadvantaged groups. Several studies, for example, show that the early interventions proposed are disproportionately more effective for socially disadvantaged.

71. The pre-school provision being extended to two- as well as three- and four-year-olds must be used to improve the social and emotional capabilities of these children and not just become another form child-minding. We must, therefore, ensure that all those working with children are adequately trained and I am aware that standards currently need to be raised.

72. The quality of the workforce is often an issue for specific programmes as well. Trained nurses, midwives or health visitors are needed for the Family Nurse Partnership, and attempts to use less qualified staff have resulted in weaker improvements.

73. A workforce development framework.

74. could establish training and salary structures which recognise the challenge and importance of early years staff and especially staff engaging with multi-problem families. Training in parent engagement would also be appropriate.

75. I believe also that we need to ensure we have a large enough workforce for the future to provide the programmes and offer childcare provision. We need to find a way to make the vocation attractive to more highly qualified candidates and we need to be encouraging schools, colleges and universities to be teaching and developing resources for the future.

Recommendations 16I recommend that we improve workforce capability with the 0-5s. We should:

- increase graduate-led, or even post-graduate, preschool leadership;

- ensure that all early years settings employ someone with Early Years Professional Status (EYPS) on site;

- establish a Workforce Development strategy led by the Departments for Education and Health with input from across government, to ensure that we are developing for the future enough suitably qualified candidates who wish to work with the 0-5s.

76. In the interim, I recommend that all key professionals are made aware of the importance of building on the social and emotional capabilities of babies and children and promoting and supporting good parenting, through refocused training this year and as an integral part of Continuous Professional Development

A national parenting campaign

77. We are seeking to change the culture about parenting and the way in which parents interaction with babies, children and young people. We have to place the role most especially of the parent at the heart of what we do. As illustrated in the earlier chapters, we know that what the child learns at home, its relationship to its parents and theirs to the child, in the earliest months or life is the single biggest influence on a child's development – more important than material circumstances or parental income, occupation or education. Indeed, the quality of a child's relationships and learning experiences in the family has more influence on achievement than innate ability, material circumstances or the quality of pre-school and school provision[21]. Yet we do next to nothing to inform parents of this and few parents and remarkably few childcare professionals have any knowledge of this. Therefore, I propose an immediate commitment by the UK Government to work with others to consider the best way to ensure that all parents can be **effective, nurturing and well informed** parents. I do not propose that this should be government funded.

This is a Big Society commitment – we all need to work together to improve our future society and this commitment should be backed by relevant experts, voluntary sector and charitable organisations, and other interested parties.

78. I believe that the government needs a strategy to change the way we in Britain conceive of parenting, to recognize that a great deal of valuable information can be taught and that all and any parents, not just those deemed to have problems, could benefit from it. Well-executed public health campaigns can be particularly effective. I believe that a national campaign would be particularly effective for this issue, where many parents have a strong desire to do the best for their children but many, especially in low income groups, are ill-informed or poorly motivated on how to achieve this. In my experience as the chair of the teenage pregnancy task force in Nottingham I have often heard the phrase "babies don't come with a handbook". It is now true that there is a plethora of material however much of it is not in a popular form or accessible through mass media.

79. The National Parenting Campaign I recommend should use the most effective ways to to make mothers, health professionals and, especially, newly pregnant women aware of the what a child needs in order that it should have healthy, stable and strong social and emotional foundations. That entails knowing how to recognise and respond to a baby's cues, attuning with infants and stimulating them from the very start, and knowing how to foster empathy. And not just that: a mother-to-be needs to understand that how she acts, how she feels, even the tone of her voice will influence the child growing inside her. All would-be and new parents need to be aware of the sensitive period for emotional development in the earliest 18 months and the particular need during that period to avoid stress, domestic violence, physical abuse and neglect. They need to appreciate the importance taking frequently with a baby, and all the things that would make a positive difference such as cuddling, looking and smiling. Parents, in particular, need to know whom to turn to for help, and where to find it. They need to know how to foster a positive learning in the home, as well as the usual information about matters breastfeeding and avoiding smoking, toxic substances and stress.

80. The government should also engage the general public in understanding the value of these principles because this would help to win a public mandate for refocusing resources and, more important, because everyone has an interest and a part to play in improving outcomes for children. I invite the government to consider this argument carefully.

Recommendation

81. I recommend a new *National Parenting Campaign* as the Crown Jewel of the Big Society project, pursued with enough passion and vitality to make it irresistible even to the most jaundiced. I recommend the creation of a broad-based alliance of interested groups, charities and foundations to ensure that the public, parents, health professionals and, especially, newly pregnant women are aware of the importance of developing social and emotional capability in the first years of life, and understand the best ways of encouraging good later outcomes for their children. Whitehall departments should participate in this initiative but not control or dominate it. For this reason, I propose that this initiative should be funded and directed from outside central government. In the interim, I recommend that specific recommendations on parenting should be published as a response to the recent consultation by the Department of Health on proposals on information for patients, service users, carers and the public.

Breaking down the barriers to provision

82. In the final half of this chapter I will prepare the ground for the key recommendations in chapters 6, 7, and 8. We examine some of the difficulties we will overcome in moving to the next stage of Early Intervention.

83. The obstacles can be overcome. Some areas are already leading the way, and throughout the text I have provided examples of areas that have put Early Intervention at the heart of their strategies. It is important that we build on this local leadership and, as Chapter 7 demonstrates, even at this very early stage 26 areas have signed the expression of interest to pioneer developments in Early Intervention.

84. However, local authorities and communities still have some way to go. Even in my home City of Nottingham, which has done more than most to focus on Early Intervention, only a third of the teenage mothers who could benefit from the Family Nurse Partnership receive that support.

85. What have been the obstacles to Early Intervention and how can these be overcome?

Political and financial barriers

86. Encouraging greater financial investment in early intervention is a crucial part of this Review, and will form the focus of the second part of recommendations later this year, as I have stated. There are a number of barriers to greater investment, which we will be considering.

87. There is clear evidence supporting the economic benefits of early intervention, and this should provide a strong basis for attracting investment from the private sector. However, there are several reasons why this is not currently being significantly achieved. These include a lack of obvious product to invest in, a lack of clear metrics on which to base financial returns, and a lack of confidence and understanding about the risks involved.

88. Additionally, the political cycle makes it harder to design a mechanism that will produce returns over a longer period required for early intervention policies to take effect. To be effective, financial instruments must protect their investors' money over a long period of time from the instability of central and local government accounting arrangements, subject as they are to changes in political priority.

89. As such external investment has largely been limited to ad hoc donations rather than larger-scale sustainable investments **This will be considered in full in the next part of the Review, including full consideration of the different types of mechanisms that could be attractive to investors.**

90. In return, politicians and other policymakers will want proof that the investment has generated the savings to budgets. There are examples of this problem starting to be dealt with in Birmingham, for example, where the results of rigorous

evaluation are tied to models that allow purchasing agencies to realise economic benefits, or similarly in Peterborough social investment bonds are being piloted. But more options are needed to reap fully the benefits of Early Intervention for children's well-being and for society generally. We need, too, to find more ways for departments and agencies to pool their budgets and share the returns on these programmes.

91. There are also financial disincentives for voluntary sector providers. Evidence-based Early Intervention policies and programmes, such as those described in the next chapter, take many years to develop, often more than 10 years and sometimes as many as 20. There is no obvious stimulus for a voluntary organisation to spend significant periods of time and resource developing a proven model by properly understanding the causes of impairments to children's health and development, rigorously evaluating their innovation, establishing procedures to ensure it can be provided consistently at scale, when central and local government will readily commission services products that do not meet any of these standards.

92. Too few innovative programmes are in a position where they can be applied more widely. Many programmes start on a relatively small scale, often trial basis, with well trained staff who understand the programme and the theory that underpins it. Providing on a larger scale is more difficult. More staff are needed and they can need high levels of training and motivation to keep the programme running with fidelity. Venture philanthropists could do more to help small programmes become better suited to wider adoption.

Choosing the right programme

93. Many examples of attempted early intervention were submitted to my Review. We set standards of evidence to decide which to recommend for future investment.

94. The general absence of robust evaluation and comparative data has greatly handicapped the progress of evidence-based Early Intervention in the UK. Without robust information on which to make comparisons, budget holders and potential investors face the problems of equivalence and accountability for outcomes.

95. The problem of equivalence refers to the way in which commissioners of Early Intervention services must choose from ill-matched options. For example, in the last decade a host of parenting programmes have emerged in the UK, but the National Academy of Parenting Practitioners – which closed in April this year- has accredited just 18[22] with far less meeting the more exacting standards applied by this Review. Without clear standards of evidence, purchasers of children's services have no clear way of making the right decision, which means that he who shouts loudest frequently gets the most attention.

Finding out about what works

96. Another obstacle standing between those who want to implement Early Interventions, which are both cost effective and based on evidence, is the limited adoption by policy makers of knowledge about "what works." There are now over 20 online sources of information on effective policy and practice for children in the areas of health, education, social care and youth justice (see Appendix [X]). There are also two internationally recognised repositories for reviews that bring together systematic reviews of the evidence (the Cochrane Collaboration for health and the Campbell Collaboration for education, crime and justice, and social welfare). The Annie E Casey Foundation and the Social Development Research Group in the U.S. have collaborated with the Social Research Unit in the U.K. to bring these sources together in a single accessible database for policy makers and practitioners, to be available from the summer of 2011.

97. Each of the above sources apply clear standards of evidence but hardly any are known to commissioners of children's services in central or local government in the UK. When major policy decisions are based on evidence, these are often restricted to departmental silos. For example, there is extensive use of information from the Cochrane Collaboration by health commissioners and practitioners but there is use of this technology into other aspects of children's development.

98. Executives who make major investment decisions on human development have limited access to reliable information about effective Early Intervention but the situation is much worse for practitioners. It is rare for university training programmes to include modules about understanding standards of evidence and working out differences between effective and ineffective interventions. In social care but not in nursing and medicine This gap is seldom rectified in the workplace. Professional magazines do not cover the literature about evidence, and it is given scant regard in many academic journals.

The Tension between proof and innovation

99. Running through this lack of attention to information about effective policy and practice is a tension between using proven models and the need to nurture innovation, especially at the local level. There is a strong history of inventiveness in services for children in the UK. Many of the staples of today's provision – for example, foster and residential care for highly disadvantaged children – have been originated and developed by strong partnerships between the voluntary and statutory sectors. In the previous administration several hundred pilots aimed at improving child well-being were sponsored by the then Department for Children, Schools and Families alone. The Centre for Excellence in Outcomes has specialised in cataloguing this innovation around the country and identifying practice that has the greatest potential to improve children's well-being.

100. However, very little UK innovation is subjected to high-quality evaluation or is prepared in such a way that it can be consistently provided in several places around the country to make such evaluation possible. Most of the policies and programmes that meet this test are international, with the majority from the US, Scandinavia and Australasia. That often raises an obvious question for purchasers of children's services and practitioners: "Why would we use something that has been shown to work in Utah when we can invent something that suits our local needs?"

Implementation

101. A further barrier to improving Early Intervention in a cost-effective way is variable and often poor implementation. There is now a strong body of evidence demonstrating that programmes for which there is strong evidence provided with low fidelity to the design of their originators generally fail to achieve their intended results. As will be seen in the following chapter, at least a dozen internationally recognised, Early Intervention programmes have now been tried in the UK but hardly any have been provided to the standards required by the programme developer. The competing demands on providers have made it commonplace to cut essential components of these programmes, particularly reducing the training requirements or not checking those skills which allow practitioners which are required by most evidence-based programmes.

102. Such behaviour is partly explained by the low volume of technical support available from those in the UK who develop programmes or specialists to advise children's services on how to get the most from the proven models they use.

103. **However, there are examples of evidence-based Early Intervention programmes being provided with fidelity in the UK. Family Nurse Partnership has reached In England, over 6,000 at Dec 10 with 7,000 by April 2011, This has been helped by the quality and coherence of the programme (its materials and training programme), the licensing requirements, the commitment of local organisations and family nurses and the leadership and support from the implementation team in the Department of Health. Judy Hutchings at the University of Bangor has provided the Incredible Years parenting programme into Welsh early years services, again with personal determination and close support of the programme developer. Birmingham have managed the strong implementation of FNP, Incredible Years, PATHS and Triple-P. This is partly due to the significant financial incentives built into the Brighter Futures programme (all savings come back to the investment team to re-invest in Early Intervention) and partly due to the technical support they received from external providers.**

104. There are conspicuous exceptions to the rule – **we discussed FNP at length and give mention of PATHS, Triple-P while also describing some in chapter 7** – but they are largely obscured by the many far less successful examples, including many supported by significant central and local government funds that have taken and badly re-assembled components from several evidence-based Early Intervention programmes or have required no checks on the quality of their implementation.

Rigorous Innovation and Evaluation

105. A final barrier to the routine use of high-quality Early Intervention has been the lack of investment in Early Intervention and prevention science in the UK. It is no accident that the majority of proven models have emerged from the US where the investment in primary research and applied sciences is far greater than in the UK. There are significant financial incentives for US scientists to seek a career developing and proving ideas to improve the lives of children and other family members. The major science funders, such as the National Institute for Health, federal government departments, such as the Department of Education, and state governments, routinely invest in experiments where the implementation is extensive. Even highly political initiatives, such as encouraging sexual abstinence in adolescence or moving families from low-income to medium-income neighbourhoods, are routinely and rigorously evaluated. No such incentives exist in the UK. The chasm between the academic and the practitioner must be bridged so that science can provide answers for Early Intervention.

106. A significant opportunity exists here. Most UK innovation starts and ends within the health, education, social care and youth justice systems that have the resources to offer extensive provision of a service. But, as has been shown, these ideas typically lack rigorous evaluation and implementation checks. Most US innovation starts, and too much of it ends, outside of the large-scale systems that can sustain the proven results at scale, also resulting in lower than anticipated levels of impact. The UK has an exceptional opportunity to provide existing and develop new evidence-based Early Intervention programmes within mainstream children's services and so reap the full potential of improvements in methodology.

107. Given the barriers to expansion, in terms of accounting, staffing and management, we need to ensure that programme and system managers have access to advice and **the funding to redesign systems on expanding operations from the public or business sector where relevant**. It is possible that this sort of advice could be provided by, or secured through, the Early Intervention Foundation.

108. There is now strong and improving evidence that certain programmes provide positive outcomes for children, young people, families and communities. But too many agencies and professionals are not aware of this evidence or do not use it.

Conclusion

109. I have made a number of specific suggestions, building on existing commitments to Early Intervention, which different bodies can take forward. But we also need increase the scale of Early Intervention so that it is available across the country. This means ensuring that we know and use the best programmes, that we have a real focus on a small number of local areas to increase the reach of the strategy, and that we create an independent institution to help central and local government take it to the next level.

110. The **following three** chapters of this report build on some of the themes that have emerged from this chapter:

111. Chapter 6 will cover the best programmes available now, to guide the choice of commissioners and help them achieve best value for money.

112. Chapter seven will focus on engaging those local areas which will become Early Intervention Places, and help them to lead by example.

113. Chapter 8 will focus on the institutional arrangements needed to create a significant change in the provision of Early Intervention, and to make evaluation, dissemination and sustainable financing a reality.

Manchester

Manchester has a strong prevention and early intervention strategy, which includes a focus on investment in these areas Their investment strategy is initially looking at:

- A core, universal offer from pre birth to 5 year olds, based on small evidence based programme of interventions;

- The identification and development of the most effective interventions to support children and young people to develop the personal skills and emotional intelligence to thrive in all circumstances;

- A Learning Transformation Programme to ensure all learning settings provide a broad educational experience that meets the needs of children and young people in Manchester.

The strategy builds on some long standing early intervention initiatives like the Children and Parents Service (CAPS), a multi-agency partnership between   Health (CAMHS), Early Years and Play, and Family Action (formerly Family Welfare Association).

CAPs aims to help parents provide the best possible environment within which their children can develop socially and emotionally to their full potential. There are two strands to this city-wide early intervention service.

1. CAPS Pre-school which provides a comprehensive range of effective interventions to parents of pre-school children and their families.

2. CAPSTIP (Children and Parents Service – Training in Partnership) supports the effective delivery of parent training programmes by other organisations.

CAPS delivers evidence-based interventions based on local need, targeted to those families most at risk.

CAPS builds on the core offer for Sure Start and Extended Schools and is monitored through high standards of audit and evaluation.

Endnotes

1   Field, F, (2010) The Foundation years: preventing poor children becoming poor adults, the report of the Independent Review on Poverty and Life Chances

2   Department of Health (2010) Healthy Lives, Healthy People, Our Strategy for Public Health in England

3   www.cqc.org.uk/aboutcqc/ involvingpeoplewhouseservices/patientsurveys/ maternityservices.cfm

4   Department of Health (2010), Healthy Lives, Healthy People, Our Strategy for Public Health in England

5   Department of Health , (2010) Healthy Lives, Healthy People, Our Strategy for Public Health in England

6   Depatrtment of Health, (2010 Health Lives, Health People: Transparency in Outcomes

7   Department of Health (2010) Liberating the NHS: legislative framework and next steps

8   Ivana La Valle, Elizabeth Clery and Mary Carmen Huerta (2008), *"Maternity Rights and Mothers' Employment Decisions. Department of Work and Pensions Research Report number 496*

9   Karoly, Lynn A,, m. Rebecca Kilburn, Jill S. Canon (2005) Early Childhood Interventions: Proven Results, Future Promise. Santa Monica, Calif.: RAND Corporation. (£34,148)

     Aos.S, Lieb. J. Mayfiekd, M. Miller & Pannucci, A. (2004) Benefits and costs of prevention and early intervention programmes for youth. Olympia: washingto State Institue for Public Policy, Document No. 04-07-3901.

10   Barnes, J et al (2008) Nurse-Family Partnership Programme: First Year Pilot Sites Implementation in England, London DCSF. www.education.gov.uk/research/data/uploadfiles/ DCSF-RW051%20v2.pdf

     Barnes, J et al (2009) Nurse-Family Partnership Programme: Implementation in England – Second Year in 10 Pilot Sites: the infancy period. London DCSF. www.education.gov.uk/research/data/uploadfiles/ DCSF-RR166.pdf

     Barnes J (2010) *forthcoming* The Family-Nurse Partnership Programme in England: Wave 1 Implementation in toddlerhood and a comparison between Waves 1 and 2a implementation in pregnancy and infancy.

11   www.triplep.net. www.incredibleyears.com

12   http://www.education.gov.uk/inthenews/inthenews/ a0070450/written-ministerial-statement-by-the-secretary-of-state-for-education-on-schools-financial-settlement-education-spending

13   Department of Education (2010), *The Importance of Teaching: The Schools White Paper 2010*. London: Department for Education.

14   Department for Education Business Plan, November 2010.

15   Evidence pack: http://www.education.gov.uk/ childrenandyoungpeople/earlylearningandchildcare/ a0070374/the-importance-of-early-years-education

16   The Foundation years: preventing poor children becoming poor adults, the report of the Independent Review on Poverty and Life Chances, Frank Field, December 2010

17   The Foundation years: preventing poor children becoming poor adults, the report of the Independent Review on Poverty and Life Chances, Frank Filed, December 2010

18   Healthy Lives, Healthy People: transparency in outcomes, proposals for a public health outcomes framework, Department of Health, 20 December 2010

19   The Effective Provision of Pre School Education (EPPE) project, Findings from Pre-School to the End of Key Stage 1, Institute of Education. Sylvia, K., Melhuish, E., Sammons, P.

20   The Effective Provision of Pre-School Education (EPPE) Project: Final Report A Longitudinal Study Funded by the DfES 1997-2004

21   The Effective Provision of Pre-School Education (EPPE) project, Findings from Pre-School to the End of Key Stage 1, Institute of Education. Sylvia, K., Melhuish, E and Sammons P.

22   Making early intervention work, Evidence submission to Allen enquiry, 25 October 2010, Stephen Scott

Chapter 6
The Programmes: A New methodology, Robust Evidence, and Backing What Works

Introduction: A New Rigour

1. One of my primary recommendations is that a greater proportion of any new public and private expenditure be spent on proven Early Intervention policies.

2. I emphasize the word "new," because I want no one reading this Review to fear for the future of existing schemes. My proposal is that any new extra funding should be used to expand programmes which have been proven to work. In this chapter I suggest which Early Intervention policies, programmes and practices should have the first claim on such funding.

3. I asked my Review team to identify the most promising Early Interventions that could be applied in the United Kingdom. Consistent with definitions in earlier chapters, they looked for interventions that could be applied before the development of impairment to a child's well-being or at an early stage of its onset, interventions which either pre-empt the problem or tackle it before it becomes entrenched and resistant to change. In examining the evidence, the Review team took into account my conclusion that the most effective Early Intervention occurs early in a child's life, but that there are also several opportunities to continue social and emotional development or to intervene early in primary and secondary school, and even in the years leading up to adulthood.

4. So in examining the evidence, the Review team were mindful of the benefits of this developmental perspective. They divided their work into Early Intervention that could be applied to all children and that which targeted specific groups or problems. These two sections are further divided

by age 0-5, 5-11, and and11-18. I have sub-divided this section in this way because of a strong belief in "prior attainment", that is, preparation for the next stage. Rather than blaming teachers and others for some failure or other we need to ensure that responsibility is taken upstream, so that measures are in place before the problem arises, not after. This is classic Early Intervention action. I define the stages as follows:

- 0-5: *Readiness for primary school.* This concept is similar to the "foundation stage", which we strongly support, in Rt Hon Frank Field's recent Review of poverty[1].By intervening early during the time from conception to the age of five we make children ready to meet all the challenges and use all the opportunities for development when they enter primary school.

- 5-11: *Readiness for secondary school.* We continue the social and emotional development already well-established by activity and intervening early during the primary school years.

- 11-18: *Readiness for life.* We continue to develop the child and young person's social and emotional skills into the teenage years and where necessary intervening before problems get entrenched. In many places, such as my constituency where 16 is the standard school leaving age, special outreach provision will be needed. We make children ready to take responsibility and achieve in adult life, especially if they become parents.

5. This framework structures the findings presented in this chapter.

6. As I have made clear in previous chapters, UK children are behind their peers in other advanced nations in many established measures of child development. I asked my team to focus on Early Intervention proposals to reduce the risk of social and emotional difficulty, because progress in these areas provides the foundation for progress in most other aspects of life.

7. I started with the ambition that both for all children and for targeted groups we should have at least one programme which we felt was proven for every age group.

8. An immediate problem for the team responding to my request is the fact that there have been thousands of responses to the problems. All are well-meaning, but too many have been reactive, waiting until problems are visible to hard-pressed child protection, child welfare or juvenile justice systems. Too few of the Early Intervention programmes currently being tried in the UK have been rigorously evaluated, making it difficult for the public sector and impossible for the private sector to invest with any confidence.

9. In order to sift through the mountain of evidence on Early Intervention, I asked my Review team to devise clear standards of evidence against which each potential policy, programme or practice could be assessed. I wanted to arrive at a situation where it was clear how the assessment was made, and for readers to be able to apply the criteria themselves and come to similar conclusions.

10. The selected standards, described below and in more detail in Appendix B, were then applied to the many thousands of examples of Early Intervention that exist internationally. The result was a list of Early Intervention programmes endorsed by many experts from around the world as reliable ways to provide the social and emotional bedrock for children that I seek. I stress once again that this is a work in progress: the list is not final, and other programmes can become included in the" most proven" category if they meet the criteria.

11. Once these evidence-based Early Intervention programmes had been selected, I asked the team to gather available information on costs and benefits, to help potential investors make sensible decisions when building an Early Intervention portfolio.

12. This chapter describes the standards used to select evidence-based Early Intervention programmes. I then describe, at each developmental stage, the kinds of Early Intervention that will begin to improve the well-being of UK children. I recognise that it will not be enough to list those proven approaches that currently make the grade, and in the concluding section I suggest how these approaches can be enhanced.

Standards of evidence

13. The Review team began with standards of evidence prepared for the Greater London Authority by the Social Research Unit at Dartington. In order to get more expert contributions, the SRU further developed the standards with the help of leading experts in the field of Early Intervention at the the Annie E. Casey Foundation, the Social Development Research Group at the University of Washington and the Blueprints for Violence Prevention Group in the United States, as well as the Institute for Effective Education in the UK.

14. The same group of experts, including Delbert Elliott, David Hawkins and Bob Slavin and their staff, were then involved in coding each potential programme against the criteria.

15. Programmes were selected using agreed criteria from staff at the Social Research Unit at Dartington working with Steve Aos at the Washington Institute of Public Policy, an acknowledged expert in this area.

16. The standards have four dimensions:

- *Evaluation quality* favouring those Early Interventions that have been evaluated to a very high standard using the most robust evaluation methods such as randomised controlled trials or quasi-experimental techniques, and ideally summarised in systematic reviews.

- *Impact* favouring those Early Interventions that have strong impact on children's health and development and particularly their social and emotional competencies.

- *Intervention specificity* favouring those Early Interventions that are clear about what they are intending to achieve, for whom, why, how and where. Much of the evaluation literature has shown clarity on this dimension to be a key characteristic of successful interventions. It is also an essential ingredient to the economic appraisal of programmes.

- *System readiness* favouring those Early Interventions that can be effectively integrated in the wider public service infrastructure and are supported by a strategy for ensuring that potential economic benefits can be realised.

17. Further explanation of the process taken to select our list, and a list of validated programmes is included in Appendix A.

18. The chart below shows how some how some of most robustly assessed interventions map across age ranges, target groups and types of provision. This does not purport to show a holistic system of early interventions, but demonstrates many interventions with proven impact are available, and in many cases have already been woven into the public service infrastructure of the UK.

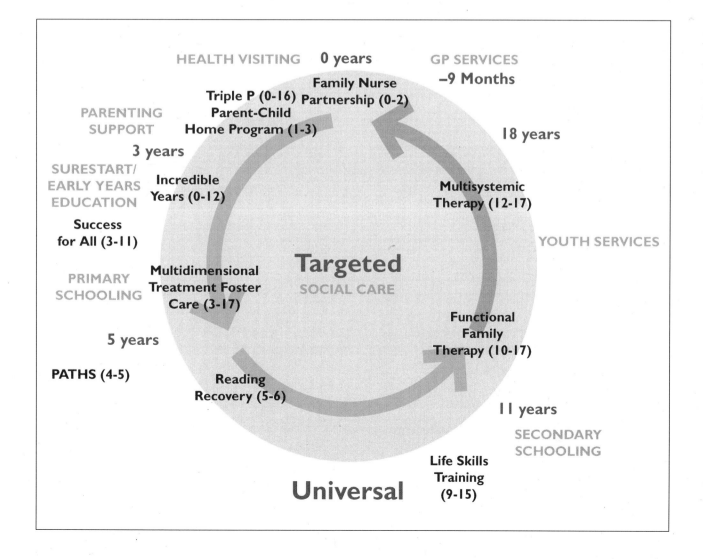

19. Given the right pathway, many excellent current UK programmes could swiftly meet these criteria and become part of the highest "proven" group.

Evidence-based Early Intervention programmes

20. Having set out how I selected evidence-based Early Intervention programmes, I can now give public and private investors examples of those which can provide the social and emotional bedrock that children need to become productive citizens. These programmes have great potential to produce future savings in public expenditure, and additional future public revenues, which could be used to guarantee a healthy return on investment. Some examples of the returns some of our proven interventions are estimated to achieve, and assessments of cost effectiveness are included in Annex C.

21. I have divided these examples into two sets. The first set represents Early Intervention for all children: policies and programmes that seek to improve outcomes for the entire child population. Many of the examples given can be thought of as a public health approach providing children with the equivalent of a social and emotional inoculation through programmes familiar in the UK such as SEAL, PATHS, PHSE and 11-16 Lifeskills.

22. The second set represents targeted Early Intervention for children in need as defined in the Children Act 1989, whose health and development is impaired or likely to become impaired without additional support. I view this as essential in breaking the cycle of deprivation that is holding back children in the most deprived communities. Targeted evidence-based Early Intervention at all stages of a child's development, but especially during the first three years of life will help 0-18s to become the good parents of tomorrow.

Evidence-based interventions for all children

23. Most children develop excellent social and emotional capabilities through the families which nurture them. Some do not and this is more (but not exclusively) likely to happen to children in low-income households with only one permanent caregiver. These children, and their caregivers, need help at the right time. Early Intervention offers the hope of social and emotional stability for every child, even in difficult circumstances.

24. The Review team's examination of the evidence revealed a class of public health Early Intervention programmes which produce improvements in the social and emotional well-being of all children. An important factor in the success of these programmes is the way in which children in a group try to be like one another in attitudes and behaviour. This means that as the well-being of the average child improves, so does the well-being of those with impairments. These programmes are provided in the community or in schools. Because they apply to every child they do not carry any of the stigmas sometimes associated with interventions that pull out children for special help.

0-5: Readiness for school: Programmes provided from conception to entry to primary school.

25. A strong evidence base assembled over many years shows how Early Intervention can better support children from conception to school. Pre-school teaching for children of two, three and four years of age has already been highlighted in this area. There is also good evidence that Sure Start children's centres contribute to improvements in child well-being in the early years in the communities in which they are provided.[2]

26. The Welsh Assembly and Birmingham City Council have demonstrated how children's centres are a valuable neutral context in which to offer advice or evidence-based programmes on parenting or relationships.

27. It is known that the availability of free or low-cost quality childcare that allows parents to go to work thus increasing household income, also makes a difference. For example, the EPPE2[3] study found benefits of high quality pre-schooling for children's intellectual, social and behavioural development at school entry, at the end of Key Stage 1 (age 7) and at Key Stage 2 (age 11).

28. The evidence on cost-benefit for this kind of provision is mixed. There is significant capital outlay to provide Sure Start-type provision and to find and train staff to work within such services. When children's centres are initially being set up the costs

are greater than the short-term benefits. However, once the initial outlay is discounted – there is now a children's centre for every community in England, as there are secondary schools, the challenge becomes how to reap the greatest benefit to children and from additional investments from the existing resource. For example, the Welsh Office has embedded the Incredible Years Parenting Programme into every children's centre. This additional programme targets children showing the early signs of conduct disorder and produces strong returns on investment.

29. Reliable cost-benefit information on Incredible Years in children's centres in the UK is being collected by the University of Bangor for Wales and the Social Research Unit for Birmingham[4].

30. From the information available at this stage of my Review, I can say that providing Incredible Years to the 150 or so three-year-olds at risk of a conduct disorder in a London borough with a child population of 35,000 would cost roughly £780,000 per year. As most experts appreciate, most of those 150 children at risk of a conduct disorder in their third year of life will, throughout childhood, be calling on child protection, special education, foster care and youth justice provisions. The figure of £780,000 is equivalent to the cost of later taking about 20 children into foster care for one year. Put another way, if Incredible Years ensures that 21 of the 150 children do not require as foster care it pays for itself, before one takes account of any other improved outcomes.

5-11: Readiness for secondary school: Programmes provided in the primary school years.

31. Early Intervention continues to be effective through the primary school years. There are many programmes that respond to early signs of failure in reading and writing skills, some of which are reviewed below. Another class of Early Intervention programme, generally but not exclusively provided in school, targets children's social and emotional regulation.

32. As we saw in chapter 2, the infant brain learns to regulate emotions and behaviour in the context of threat, disappointment and general discomfort. Put simply, when a child cannot understand a school problem or is pushed by a

fellow pupil in the playground their brain must process the challenge and decide how to react. When regulation is poor the response tends to be counter-productive, for example giving up on the school problem or hitting out at the pupil in the playground. When regulation is strong, better emotional and behavioural reactions follow.

33. A class of social and emotional regulation programmes, summarised on the Collaborative for Academic, Social and Emotional Learning website, exposes children to a series of routines that improve the brain's regulation of emotions.[5] Put plainly, these routines gradually increase the milliseconds between stimulus and reaction, meaning that children have more time to think of an appropriate response.

34. Joseph Durlak and colleagues at Loyola University of Chicago systematically reviewed the evidence from over 500 rigorous evaluations of social and emotional regulation programmes involving over 200,000 primary school children.[6] They found significant effects on children's emotions and ordinary behaviours such as lying, stealing, cheating and not paying attention. Although most social and emotional regulation programmes do not target academic performance, on average they produce improvements in reading and writing equivalent to taking a class from the 50th percentile to the 61st percentile. Happier, better-behaved children learn more.

35. The experience of implementing social and emotional regulation programmes in the UK has been mixed. There are good examples in Northern Ireland, Birmingham and Norfolk of implementing Promoting Alternative Thinking Strategies (PATHS) with fidelity. PATHS is a curriculum- supported by school-wide activities that is provided in one hour's worth of lessons each week. Early results from experimental evaluations of these programmes are promising, and information about the cost-benefits will come from the Birmingham trial.

36. The Social and Emotional Aspect of Learning (SEAL) programme is an amalgam of several evidence-based approaches provided nationwide. The variable provision of SEAL possibly accounts for the less optimistic findings reported by Neil Humphrey, Ann Lendrum and Michael

Wigelsworth at the University of Manchester[7]. Nonetheless, the SEAL initiative has given schools permission to invest in evidence-based social and emotional programmes, and early results from Northern Ireland and Birmingham **SOMETHING MISSING HERE?**. If SEAL meets the criteria above there is no reason it cannot be one of the proven programmes.

37. The rigorous evaluation of PATHS in Birmingham was in the process of being reported as the first stage of my Review went to press. The early results demonstrate significant reductions in conduct disorders consistent with the Durlak research quoted above. If this evidence-based Early Intervention programme were provided to every child aged five to seven in primary schools in a Northern city with a child population of 160,000 the cost would be about £800,000 a year, the cost of taking about 22 children into foster care for one year. In the second part of my Review I will be able to offer sophisticated cost-benefit analyses on programmes like PATHS. However, if the results of Joseph Durlak and Birmingham can be replicated I find it inconceivable that this Early Intervention would fail to keep fewer than 22 children out of state care. Again, this takes no account of other improved outcomes which would reduce the need for high-cost reactive provision.

11-18: Readiness for life: Programmes provided in the secondary school years.

38. The Review led me to understand that the social and emotional foundations built in babies, pre-schoolers and at primary level should be reinforced during the secondary school years. There are evidence-based Early Intervention programmes for adolescents, helping them to make and sustain relationships and how to make sensible decisions about their future lives. Evidence-based programmes in this category typically take the form of additions or amendments to school curricula. These can last from a few weeks to several years, and are sometimes supplemented by activities for parents and changes to the school environment. All target known risk factors, all of which strongly feature in UK society.

39. Age-appropriate social and emotional skills help young people make good choices in life. They may teach young people what it means

to make and sustain relationships and to have a baby. The right assertiveness skills can help them resist pressure from others of their own age and fashionable influences and so not to behave stupidly and destructively. They can also build adolescents' self-confidence and help them to manage their emotions positively, since individuals often act up when they are unhappy or confused.

40. Other current approaches are based on providing reliable information about, for example, the consequences of drug misuse or risk of infection for sexually transmitted infections, with the aim of curbing favourable or careless attitudes towards risky behaviours. Changing beliefs about what is considered acceptable or normal behaviour is another approach that is particularly powerful in adolescence: it is easier to say "no" to doing something if you do not believe that your peers are doing it. Last, many programmes place a strong emphasis on building communication skills, so that young people can express how they are feeling and not become estranged from potential prosocial figures in their lives, especially their parents.[8]

41. Unfortunately, there has been a tendency for UK schools to develop their own substance misuse and life skills programmes rather than use proven models like Life Skills Training (LST) which are known to improve outcomes for children.

42. LST is currently provided to about 20 per cent of adolescents in schools in the USA. It prevents the initiation of tobacco, alcohol and marijuana use, and other gateway drugs during adolescence. The curriculum comprises 30 lessons provided by classroom teachers in schools over a three-year period. The classes reduce individual vulnerability and foster resistance to the social influences such as media, family and friends known to contribute to the use of gateway drugs.

43. Accordingly, LST helps young people to develop self-management skills, including decision-making and coping with anxiety, and social skills, including communication. Several rigorous evaluations have shown that LST cuts tobacco, alcohol and marijuana use by between 50 and 75 per cent.[9] Results are sustained for about six years, meaning that there is also decreased the use of inhalants, narcotics and hallucinogens that are more common in late adolescence. The cost

of providing LST to every child aged 11 to 13 in a large county with 200,000 children would be less than £2 million a year.

44. Steve Aos from the Washington State Institute for Public Policy reliably informs me that £1 spent on LST will generate more than £25 of savings. His work with the Social Research Unit at Dartington and UK local authorities will validate this figure by the time the second part of my Review is complete. But even on extremely conservative and restrictive assumptions which reduce Steve Aos's figure by a factor of four, LST in the large county would still generate savings to education, social care and youth justice agencies of about £8 million a year.

Targeted early interventions

45. Early Intervention also works by targeting children showing the early signs of impairments to health and development, including mental health disorders. Typically, these programmes use a measurement instrument to screen families who may be having difficulty. For example, the Incredible Years programme in Birmingham children's centres is provided to mothers of children aged 3 and 4 who score highly on a 25-item measure developed in the UK called the Strengths and Difficulties Questionnaire (SDQ). This rapid reporting by mothers reliably picks out children who are showing early signs of a conduct disorder, significant emotional problems or hyperactivity.

46. Using scientifically validated tools allows practitioners to approach families and offer them the help they need before their problems get out of hand. It stands in contrast to waiting for problems to accumulate until families knock on the door of hard pressed local services and generally find problems are deep rooted and can only be expensively mitigated and managed rather than resolved.

47. Early Intervention can be targeted at just about every problem which now requires a response from modern health, policing and children's services agencies: behavioural and emotional problems, failure to perform well in school, poor parenting (including child protection challenges and major dysfunction in

relationships), and anti-social behaviour (including crime). It is worth repeating that breaking the cycle of dysfunctional behaviour helps not only the individual child but stops the replication of dysfunction in succeeding generations.

0-5: Readiness for school: Programmes provided from conception to primary school entry

48. Targeted Early Intervention in the early years tends to mix a focus on deep structures in parent-child relationships, such as attachment and coercive parenting, with attention to practical problems of income or support with reading and writing. The importance of attachment has been stressed in earlier chapters. The bonding of an infant to his or her mother and other family members provides the security to meet the challenges throughout childhood and into adulthood. Early Intervention programmes like Family Nurse Partnership build attachment. Coercive parenting refers to the process whereby parents give as much or even more attention to their children's negative behaviour as they do to their children's positive behaviour. Such attention, much sought after by all children, especially in infancy, has the opposite effect from that sought by the parent, because it rewards poor behaviour. Several Early Intervention programmes like Incredible Years teach parents how to avoid coercive parenting and reward positive behaviour instead.

49. Programmes like Parent-Child Home align these ideas with help for parents to get their children ready for school. The programme uses trained para-professionals to work with families who have not had access to educational and economic opportunities. The para-professionals stress the importance of parent-child interaction and verbal stimulation of the infant brain. Like many targeted evidence-based programmes, Parent-Child Home stresses the value of "modelling" – demonstrating to parents how to play with their child and enjoy his or her development – rather than teaching skills in class.

50. One of the leading evidence-based Early Intervention programmes in the world is Nurse Family Partnership, provided in the UK as Family Nurse Partnership. This programme focuses on first-time vulnerable (often teenage) mothers. A trained health visitor is given additional skills to

provide expectant mothers with the deep support to form strong attachments with their child and to avoid damaging parenting techniques. The intervention also provides practical support, getting mothers back into work and giving them the insight and the skills to delay subsequent pregnancies. This increases household income and boosts parental aspirations.

51. During the preparation of the Review, Government announced that FNP would be expanded from 5,000 vulnerable mothers to over 12,000, a development I wholeheartedly welcome.

52. I repeat from chapter 5 my recommendation that this programme should be offered to *all* the 60,000 parents meeting the criteria used by FNP. My confidence in this assertion is backed by personal discussions with its founder Professor David Olds. I am also convinced by the quality of the evidence base, including the largest worldwide trial currently under way in the UK; by the significant economic benefits reported by the Washington State Institute for Public Policy; and by the fact that the benefits are felt at different developmental stages. In the early years, they appear as better mother-child relationships; in the primary school years as better school performance; in secondary school as reduced anti-social behaviour better emotional health; and in adulthood as reduced likelihood teenage pregnancy in the next generation.

53. In the second part of the Review, I will be able to give more precise estimates of the costs and benefits of FNP. From the information currently to hand, my team estimates that providing 60,000 places (and many will choose not to take it up) across the country would cost about £360 million a year – about the same as providing 150,000 foster care placements in which we invest each year . I am confident, from the evidence already existing that conservatively the benefits to the taxpayer of this investment would be in the region of £1 billion a year in reduced need for foster places and other high-cost later interventions.

5-11 readiness for secondary school: Programmes provided in the primary school years.

54. Running across the categories of Early Intervention described in this chapter are programmes that target children who are showing, or likely to show, the first signs of struggling with school-related tasks, especially core challenges with reading and writing. All too frequently the field of education has been stuck between contrasting ideological standpoints, masking the availability of evidence-based approaches to tackle basic problems faced by a minority of school children.

55. I believe that given the right assistance several excellent UK programmes could meet our criteria to be "proven". The most pervasive programme, still little taken up in the UK, is Success for All, developed at Johns Hopkins University in the USA and supported by the Institute of Effective Education at the University of York.[10] Success for All starts from the premise that, in the absence of an organic disability, every child should be able to read. The programme screens out primary school pupils who are struggling readers and facilitates a range of interventions that prevent the student giving up on basic English skills. (The programme has been adapted for pre-school settings also.) The intensity of the intervention is gauged to ensure that all participants quickly rise to a level at which they can benefit from ordinary high quality classroom instruction.

56. Results from a series of high-quality evaluations show that, compared with control groups, Success for All schools have higher achievement, with better reading achievement (including among English language learners) and fewer students assigned to special education or having to repeat grades.[11] In a series of studies involving more than 6,000 students over 10 years, students in Success for All schools were on average a full grade level ahead of those in similar control schools by fifth grade (end of primary school), a difference that was maintained into early adolescence even though the intervention was finished.[12]

11-18: ready for life: Programmes provided in the secondary school years.

57. In recent years, a range of Early Intervention programmes, for which there is evidence of efficacy, have emerged as a genuine alternative to unproven and potentially damaging traditional responses to adolescent difficulty, such as taking children into foster or residential care. Behaviour modification techniques that reward desisting from bad conduct and display of good actions are usually at the core of these interventions. However, the huge physical and developmental transitions of adolescence generally require much attention to relationships alongside practical support to keep the young person in question engaged in ordinary life, going to school, engaged in other activities and beginning to think about work and further education. Effective interventions usually target parents as well as children.

58. Screening for Early Intervention in adolescence generally picks out young people with significant problems. Some evidence-based programmes in this category, like Multi-dimensional Treatment Foster Care, currently being trialled in the UK, involve placement away from home for short periods.

59. Functional Family Therapy (FFT), currently being trialled in Brighton, focuses on young people aged 11-18 years who display the early symptoms of repeated criminal behaviour, including violence. The programme is rooted in evidence that family conflict, poor family management practices, academic failure and parental drug use and crime are among the risk factors that produce anti-social behaviour. FFT builds protective factors such as parent-child bonding, positive communication and skills to resist anti-social influences. As its name suggests, FFT is aimed at parents as well as their adolescent children. A qualified social worker is given further training to provide 30 hours of treatment involving both parents and the young person, with a focus on re-framing relationship difficulties – stopping blaming interactions amongst other elements, that are driving the child's anti-social behaviour. This highly structured and closely supervised training is supplemented by other support, such as job training and help with learning difficulties.

60. Multiple evaluations have shown that FFT, provided with fidelity, reduces criminal recidivism, out-of-home placement or referral of other adolescents in the family for extra help from children's services by between 25 per cent and 55 per cent.[13] The programme is also proven to prevent adolescents with behaviour or drug use disorders from entering more restrictive and services, which also cost more.

61. A typical London borough with 35,000 children might expect to have 500 children in foster care, mostly adolescents. The cost of these foster placements will be about £18 million a year. Providing FFT as an alternative to foster care for 100 of these children would cost about £200,000, an annual saving of about £3.5 million. The economic benefits of foster care are not reported. But I am confident from the information already at hand [SPECIFY PL] that each 100 FFT places would generate savings to the Exchequer and benefits to the individual children of about £425,000, and my colleague Steve Aos at the Washington State Institute for Public Policy would calculate nearer £1.5 million.

62. I realise that in a series of examples I have suggested that programmes can save money by reducing the need for foster care. I do not wish to disparage foster care, still less the foster parents who are providing an essential service for society. But the fact remains that fostering is an expensive option and it is also true that many fostering services, whether local authority, independent or voluntary, are now under great pressure. It makes every kind of financial and social sense to reduce the number of children in need of foster care.

How I envisage this list of programmes being used

63. This list of programmes has been assembled quickly. It is the product of the work by some of the world's leading experts in Early Intervention and evidence-based programmes. But I do not see it as the last word. On the contrary, I see it as the first word.

64. There is sufficient evidence here for communities and local authorities that wish to begin the process of improving Early Intervention, particularly the places that I describe in more

depth in the next chapter, to begin to select and implement programmes from the list. But I also wish the list to be developed in several ways. In chapter 9, I recommend the establishment of an independent Early Intervention Foundation. I see the Foundation taking a lead role in the following proposed developments:

Validating standards

65. I recommend that the Early Intervention Foundation re-validate the standards of evidence used to select programmes for my Review. This process will involve further consultation with central and local government purchasers of children's services, local providers of services, including the voluntary sector, and scientists. My hope is that there will be broad agreement around a high standard of evidence for Early Intervention. Our children deserve nothing less.

Charting the route from innovation to evidence

66. Readers will have noticed that many of the programmes selected by the Review team have their origins outside of the U.K., mostly in the United States. This does not reflect any lack of innovation in the field of Early Intervention in this country. On the contrary, during the Review and in the preparation of my book with Iain Duncan-Smith[14], I have been constantly impressed with the potential for voluntary and statutory organisations to develop ingenious ideas to help our children. But we have lagged behind other countries in the rigorous development and testing of those ideas.

67. Appendix E comprises a diagram taken from the Greater London Authority's Standards of Evidence document. It describes the steps involved in moving from an original idea to intervene early to improve children's social and emotional capacity. It shows how greater attention to questions of intervention specificity being clearer about who will be served, for how long, at what cost, and with what objective will lead to a stronger Early Intervention. It sets out how agencies can better evaluate their ideas at successive stages of development, with the goal of eventually improving beyond reasonable doubt the benefits to children and to public finances of their policy, programme or practice. It describes the steps needed to make a good idea ready for wider implementation, so

that once proven it can be routinely provided by education, social care, health, and youth justice agencies.

68. The Social Research Unit at Dartington have been commissioned to prepare a longer publication that will guide Early Intervention innovators to the highest standards of evidence described in this Review. I welcome this publication and would like to see it developed by the Early Intervention Foundation. I recommend that Foundation funds are put aside to help prove the most promising, but as yet untested of UK Early Interventions.

69. My ambition is that, in five years time, the list of evidence-based Early Intervention programmes supported by the new foundation will number as many UK-born contributions as those developed overseas.

From lower leagues to the "Premiership". Promoting innovation.

There is ever broader acceptance of the benefits of high standards of proof. Now that resources are scarce, and if we are to achieve my ambition of additional public and private investment in Early Intervention, it is necessary to have in place the highest degree of certainty on programme effectiveness. I am mindful, however, that the rich seam of UK innovation, including some I have sponsored in my own City of Nottingham, should feel inspired, not inhibited, by higher standards.

• As I describe later, one of the roles of the new Early Intervention Foundation described in chapter 8 will be to assist UK agencies to navigate the route from good idea to proven model. What would be involved? I have thought about this in the context of one programme from Nottingham that I was personally involved in and greatly value, the City's 11-16 Life Skills Programme. This programme is designed to strengthen the social and emotional capabilities of teenagers and is up and running in all Nottingham's secondary schools. It synthesises the best in PHSE, SRE, Secondary SEAL, and other programmes, and helped form the proposals in the last Children's Bill which fell with the advent of the 2010 general election.

• The starting point for further developing this excellent programme will be to improve its Intervention specificity. We need to be clearer about what my colleagues on the Nottingham Life Skills Programme are intending to achieve, for whom, why, how and where. Getting this clearer will help to be more specific about costs, which later will support the analysis of costs and benefits that will be required. We would strongly advise that all new programmes build in adequate evaluation costs from the outset.

• The second stage will be to test the Programme with a more rigorous evaluation. Like many UK early intervention programmes, Nottingham Life Skills has been evaluated many times, always with promising results, but it will need to use a method, such as Randomised Controlled Trial, to meet the standards of evidence used in my Review devised by internationally renowned practitioners such as Del Elliott and Steve Aos.

• This evaluation would produce the specific estimate of impact children's social and emotional health that is fundamental to the kind of economic analysis required for public and private sectors to feel confident about investing. What the Nottingham Lifeskills programme currently lacks, in common with many other excellent UK designed early interventions, is an 'effect size', which the economists can plug into their models used in advising investors about where to get the best return of their scarce resources.

• The final stage of work will be to ensure that the programme is 'system ready', meaning that it can be provided routinely by statutory agencies with the support of local voluntary organisations. Unlike our colleagues in the United States who have excelled in high quality evaluation but struggle to prepare products that can be provided systematically, my colleagues in Nottingham and elsewhere in the UK will excel at this task.

• Given the considerable development work already complete, I would expect Nottingham 11-16 Lifeskills not only to continue to do excellent work but with the support of the Early Intervention Foundation described in Chapter X to meet all of the high standards of evidence which I advocate within three years-a blink of an eye in the period of the intergenerational change we are trying to achieve. During my scrutiny for this Review I have come across dozens of excellent UK innovations ready to make this important journey. I am convinced that within five years the UK if motivated by an independent Foundation can become the focal point of evidence based early intervention in the world.

Information on cost-benefits

70. Many of the programmes in the list developed by my Review produce substantial economic benefits to local authorities, to central government and to individuals. However, the metrics for assessing costs and benefits remain varied, and have deterred me from publishing too much information in this first stage of my Review. In some cases, there is no information at all.

71. I have been fortunate enough to work closely with Birmingham and Manchester city councils together with the Greater London Authority who are funding a project to translate the Washington State Institute for Public Policy economic model for use in the UK. Once complete, this open source software, will allow any provider of a properly evaluated Early Intervention programme to calculate the costs and benefits of the approach. I do not see this model as the only way to calculate costs and benefits, but I am impressed by the conservative nature of its estimates and its relevance to day to day investment decisions by local and central government (and later private) investors in Early Intervention. I am excited by the way the model has been used by government in the US to inform major policy decisions.

72. I recommend that the Early Intervention Foundation apply this econometric model to calculate the costs and benefits of every Early Intervention programme that passes the re-validated standards of evidence. This reliable economic information will be invaluable not least to the places identified in the next chapter who may wish to build a portfolio of Early Intervention.

Implementation

73. More or less every expert I talked to during the preparation of my review reminded me of the penalties of failure to implement these evidence-based Early Intervention programmes with fidelity to the design of their originators. This typically results in the loss of all their potential impact, economic gains as well as to child well-being. The UK has a poor track record in fidelity of implementation.

74. I have been impressed by the work of Jane Barlow at the University of Warwick in cataloguing the features of effectively implemented programmes. She talks about good programme design and content, including making sure it has sufficient dosage and intensity. This refers to the timing and socio-cultural relevance of programmes. She points out the need for well qualified, trained and supportive staff who can foster good relationships with children and families. There is also a need for continuous programme assessment and quality assurance.

75. My charge to the independent Early Intervention Foundation will be to provide support for the rigorous implementation of evidence based Early Intervention programmes.

Summary

76. Much of what has been said above appears technical in nature. However, its motivation is simple - to ensure that many more of our nation's children grow up with the social and emotional bedrock that will enable them to be the great parents and better citizens of tomorrow. Using rigorous methodology and clear criteria has moved this from well meaning aspiration to a tough practical policy. This gives us the prospect of not only taking proven policies to scale but of having the strength of evidence to attract private as well as public financing.

77. If our country is to take this to the next level we need experienced and willing local organisations to pioneer it. I turn to that in our next chapter.

Endnotes

1 Field, F, (2010), The Foundation Years: preventing poor children becoming poor adults, Independent Review of Poverty and Life Chances, HM Government

2 Sylva, K. Melhuish, E. Sammons, P. Siraj-Blatchford, I, Taggart, B. (2004), The Effective Provision of Preschool Education project: Final Report

3 Sylva, K. Melhuish, E. Sammons, P. Siraj-Blatchford, I, Taggart, B. (2004), The Effective Provision of Preschool Education project: Final Report from the Primary Phase: Pre-school, School and Family Influences on Children's Development During Key Stage 2 (Age 7-11), DCSF Research Report 061

4 Implementation of Birmingham's Brighter Future's Strategy, The Social Research Unit, Available here: http://www.dartington.org.uk/birmingham-brighter-futures

5 www.casel.org. See also: CASEL (2003) Safe and Sound: An Educational Leader's Guide to Evidence-Based Social and Emotional Learning (SEL) Programs, Chicago, IL: Collaborative for Academic, Social and Emotional Learning.

6 Payton, J., Weissberg, R. P., Durlak, J. A., Dymnicki, A. B., Taylor, R. D., Schellinger, K. B. & Pachan, M. (2008) The Positive Impact of Social and Emotional Learning for Kindergarten to Eighth-Grade Students: Findings from Three Scientific Reviews. Chicago, IL: Collaborative for Academic, Social, and Emotional Learning.

7 Humphry, N. Lendrum, A. Wigelsworth, M. (2010) Social and Emotional Aspects of Learning (SEAL) Programme in Secondary Schools: National Evaluation, Department for Education Research Report 049

8 For example: Eisen, M., Zellman, G. L., Massett, H. A., & Murray, D. M. (2002). Evaluating the lion's-quest "Skills for adolescence" Drug education program: First-year behavioral outcomes. Addictive Behaviors, 27, 619-632; Foshee, V. A., Linder, G. F., Bauman, K. E., Langwick, S. A., Arriaga, X. B., Heath, J. L., et al. (1996). The Safe Dates project: Theoretical basis, evaluation design, and selected baseline findings. American Journal of Preventive Medicine, 12(Suppl. 2), 39-47; Coyle, K.K., Kirby, D., Parcel, G., Basen-Engquist, K., Banspach, S., Rugg, D., & Weil, M. (1996). Safer Choices: A multi-component school-based HIV/STD and pregnancy prevention program for adolescents. Journal of School Health, 66(3), 89-94; Werch, C. E., Anzalone, D. M., Brokiewicz, L. M., Felker, J., Carlson, J. M., & Castellon-Vogel, E. A. (1996). An intervention for preventing alcohol use among inner-city middle school students. Archives of Family Medicine, 5(3), 146-152.

9 Many of the evaluations of LST are summarised in Botvin, G.J., Mihalic, S.F., & Grotpeter, J.K. (1998). Life Skills Training: Blueprints for Violence Prevention, Book Five. Blueprints for Violence Prevention Series (D.S. Elliott, Series Editor). Boulder, CO: Center for the Study and Prevention of Violence, Institute of Behavioral Science, University of Colorado. See for example: Botvin, G. J. (1989). The Effectiveness of a Multicomponent Skills Training Approach to Substance Abuse Prevention (Final Report Contract #C001531). New York: Cornell University Medical College, Laboratory of Health Behavior Research; Botvin, G. J., Baker, E., Dusenbury, L., Tortu, S., and Botvin, E. M. (1990). Preventing adolescent drug abuse through a multimodal cognitive-behavioral approach: Results of a 3-year study. Journal of Consulting and Clinical Psychology, 58, 437-446; Botvin, G. J., Baker, E., Dusenbury, L., Botvin, E. M., and Diaz, T. (1995). Long-term follow-up results of a randomized drug abuse prevention trial in a white middle-class population. JAMA, 273, 1106-1112.

10 www.successforall.org.uk

11 Borman, G., Slavin, R.E., Cheung, A., Chamberlain, A., Madden, N.A., & Chambers, B. (2007). Final reading outcomes of the national randomized field trial of Success for All. American Educational Research Journal, 44 (3), 701-731; Borman, G. D. & Hewes, G. M. (2003) 'The long-term effects and cost-effectiveness of Success for All', Educational Evaluation and Policy Analysis 24, 243-267.

12 Borman, G. D. & Hewes, G. M. (2003) 'The long-term effects and cost-effectiveness of Success for All', Educational Evaluation and Policy Analysis 24, 243-267.

13 Many of the evaluations of FFT are summarised in Alexander, J., Barton, C., Gordon, D., Grotpeter, J., Hansson, K., Harrison, R., Mears, S., Mihalic, S., Parsons, B., Pugh, C., Schulman, S., Waldron, H., & Sexton, T. (1998). Functional Family Therapy: Blueprints for Violence Prevention, Book Three. Blueprints for Violence Prevention Series (D.S. Elliott, Series Editor). Boulder, CO: Center for the Study and Prevention of Violence, Institute of Behavioral Science, University of Colorado. For example: Alexander, J.F., & Parsons, B.V. (1973). Short term behavioral intervention with delinquent families: Impact on family process and recidivism. Journal of Abnormal Psychology, 81, 219-225; Barton, C., Alexander, J. F., Waldron, H., Turner, C. W., & Warburton, J. (1985). Generalizing treatment effects of Functional Family Therapy: Three replications. American Journal of Family Therapy, 13, 16-26; Friedman, A.S. (1989). Family therapy vs. parent groups: Effects on adolescent drug abusers. American Journal of Family Therapy, 17, 335-347.

14 Allen, G. and Smith, I-D (2008), Early Intervention: Good parents, Great Kids. Centre for Social Justice and the Smith Institute.

Chapter 7
The Places: Pioneers for a New Way

We to-day's procession heading, we the route for travel clearing,
Pioneers! O pioneers!

Walt Whitman 1819-1892

Introduction

1. This chapter links the best Early Intervention programmes, described in the previous chapter, with the most effective public agencies, local councils and voluntary groups. The last 15 years have seen many individual steps towards improved Early Intervention but, nationally, we are still some way from achieving either the scale or the balance of provision needed. This chapter reviews some of the stronger initiatives in specific places and examines ways in which the UK can use them to shift toward an Early Intervention culture. Local councils have been incredible innovators in this field and, working with partners, they must be, with full political and official backing, the vehicle for the advance of Early Intervention. In this chapter I look at some of the excellent local innovation and suggest ways in which we can build on this progress. This country now has a patchy understanding of the benefits of Early Intervention and, with it, patchy provision. We now have a real opportunity to move to consistent Early Intervention approaches and strategies implemented on the basis of solid evidence of their impact, cost savings and other benefits, and in so doing add still more to the evidence base.

Developments since 2000

2. Early Intervention has received considerable investment since the turn of the new century. This is well illustrated by the Sure Start children's centres in disadvantaged communities in England and the family intervention services which are now part of the provision of almost all local authorities in England. As I described in the last chapter, evaluations demonstrate benefits in several areas of children's pre-school development and children's centres provide an excellent context for evidence-based Early Intervention programmes.

3. However, criticisms can also be levelled against national investments in Early Intervention over the last decades. There has been much change and it has proved hard to distinguish success from failure. The scale and number of initiatives have been associated with a variable quality of implementation. As I indicated at the end of the previous chapter, it is now well known that lack of fidelity – sticking rigorously to the discipline and measures of a programme – significantly erodes the impact of evidence-based Early Intervention. Moreover, the periods allocated for funding have generally been too short, with the result that attempts to support programme implementation, such as the National Academy for Parenting Practitioners, have been short-lived.

The NAPP closed, after three years, in April 2010. In sum, public expenditure has not been spent strategically, has *not* developed a core of successful Early Intervention policy, and above all, has *not* arrested the decline in the social and emotional development of UK children during recent decades.

4. A change of government allows senior political leaders a rare opportunity to take a new approach with a fundamental rebalancing to Early Intervention. As I made clear in my book with Iain Duncan-Smith, I view this commitment as cross party.[1] I recognise the potential to build on foundations laid by the previous administration. It is also clear that in the future, without threatening any existing programmes, a number of new initiatives – not the plethora we have had in the past – would allow better implementation, more rapid learning and a sharper focus on successful Early Intervention. The balance between centrally directed and locally directed initiatives also requires review. Local people, organisations and systems are best placed to assess the needs of local children and families and draw on a choice of proven programmes. Advice on assessment, the merits of different types of investment, and evaluation options could still be provided centrally but Whitehall could find advantages in not performing this role itself.

Local Innovation

5. I took evidence from local agencies and authorities in England, Wales Scotland and Northern Ireland. The short timescales did not permit a comprehensive assessment of local innovation, nor is the role of the Review to report all of the interesting initiatives that have come to the notice of the Review team. The Centre for Excellence and Outcomes in Children and Young People's Services has been cataloguing and validating emerging good practice across the country and is a more reliable source of interesting local initiatives. I have restricted myself in this section to a handful of the many hundreds of examples I could have included.

6. A number of local authorities have been finding ways of better screening, assessing and identifying families with children showing the first signs of impaired health and development. There are several examples of this approach to Early Intervention in the capital. The Tower Hamlets Social Inclusion Panel, with representatives from health, police, social and pupil services, decides on packages of support to be offered to the 80 most troubled children and young people each year. Selected cases are assigned a lead professional from within the panel to co-ordinate an integrated package of services. In Wandsworth, multi agency panels backed up by strong data on local need, serve a similar purpose, as do information hubs in Kingston-upon-Thames. Croydon is using its involvement in the Community Budget initiative – described below – to achieve more accurate identification of early social and emotional vulnerabilities in children who come to the attention of health and social care agencies and schools. Croydon plans to extend screening to detect problems with attachment, motor skills, speech and language difficulties, as well as emotional and behavioural issues. Away from London, in East Sussex, disadvantaged communities and families in Hastings and Rother are served by integrated health and Sure Start children's centres with joint leadership across the NHS and local authority. Family Nurse Partnerships is a core programme within their mainstream services with a strong voice for local parents through innovative Sure Start children's centre provision.

7. A second set of initiatives is focusing on the most damaged families within a jurisdiction, with the goal of giving a better chance to the next generation of children. One of the strongest examples is the Dundee Intensive Family Support programme, developed by Action for Children. This model has also been adopted in England, where there are now around 300 projects providing support for families with multiple problems. Families are given enduring and intensive support, including individual and couple therapy, parenting support and specialist support for problems like substance misuse. The Family Recovery Programme in Westminster is an example of this kind of project and co-ordinates a range of interventions for the highest-risk families.

Westminster City Council's Family Recovery Programme focuses on treating the root causes of social breakdown rather than dealing only with its symptoms. This "whole family" approach to intervention recognises the inter-relationship of the causes and effects of social breakdown. For instance, it recognises that poor housing and parental drug use are likely to lead to poor health and a lack of educational achievement for children. The programme has developed an innovative "cost-avoidance" methodology. With the council as the lead partner, the FRP brings together a number of public services, as well as national and local voluntary groups, to share resources, intelligence and expertise, and provide a single focus for dealing with the deep-rooted problems suffered by the individual families concerned. The expertise provided by Team around the Family comprises:

- adult mental health

- adult substance misuse

- neighbourhood and youth policing

- anti-social behaviour teams

- housing advice

- debt, budgeting and benefits advice

- intensive outreach work to engage hard to reach families

- parenting and life skills

- domestic violence (separate specialists in perpetrators and victims)

- education

- child health

- information analysis

- preparation for and access to training, volunteering and work.

The TAF receives referrals from a wide range of statutory and non-statutory organisations. It acts as a single unit, based in one location, and reports directly to a single operational head. TAF members share information from their respective services in a unique way, overcoming agency barriers to provide coherent and consistent action. Integrated support is provided early to young siblings. The TAF seeks a family's consent prior to intervention – except in cases where crime and children's safeguarding are of critical importance and thus override data protection legislation – in a clear and commonsense way. It sets clear and achievable goals and is honest about the consequences for those individuals who fail radically to improve their behaviour.

8. Several local authorities and voluntary organisations have made contributions through the rigorous implementation of evidence-based programmes described in the previous chapter. Birmingham has introduced programmes across all stages of child development, including Family Nurse Partnership, Incredible Years, PATHS and Triple-P. Brighton has led the way with Functional Family Therapy as an alternative to foster care and youth justice provision. Save the Children is promoting Families and School Together (FAST), an Early Intervention evidence-based programme partly developed and fully tested in the UK.[2] This programme supports parents of children aged three to five and builds community support for families. The benefits are measured in terms of children's social and emotional well-being and readiness for school. Save the Children selected FAST because of its robust evidence base4 and because of its potential to close the early years achievement gap and to remedy the lack of voluntary, first-engagement family services in the UK. Save the Children is now working with a range of local authorities to model different ways that FAST can be more widely implemented and sustained within their spectrum of local services. The aim is to establish 400 new FAST groups by 2014.

9. Other local authorities have sought a comprehensive approach to the problem of Early Intervention. One Nottingham is the local strategic planning partnership that brings together public, private, community and voluntary sector representatives in Nottingham. It has succeeded in putting Early Intervention at the heart of all its services. With Birmingham and Wales, Nottingham has been at the forefront of attempts to rebalance public expenditure towards Early Intervention with the goal of decreasing future demand for costly specialist services and thus enabling them to focus on the most difficult cases.

"Our aim is to break the intergenerational nature of under-achievement and deprivation in Nottingham by identifying at the earliest possible opportunity those children, young people, adults and families who are likely to experience difficulty and to intervene and empower people to transform their lives and their future children's lives."
Ian Curyer, Director of Children's Services, Nottingam City

This Early Intervention approach is focusing on:

- Tackling intergenerational issues
- Those activities that, if delivered effectively, can reduce the
- number of specialist interventions
- Bringing partner resources together
- Targeting work at those individuals or families who are very
- likely to have difficulties without effective intervention
- (This is subtly different to prevention which is targeted at those
- individuals/families who might have difficulties);
- Coherence for the children, young people and
- families within the delivery model;
- Shifting resources to tackle the complex causes of problems, rather than just treating the symptoms

Early effective support is given priority through:

- Establishing in Nottingham a small number of critical, evidence-based, Early Interventions for specific stages in childhood, making them sustainable, and using them as a blueprint for service development
- Shifting greater resources into prevention and Early Intervention and exploring
- the cost and benefits of specific interventions
- Reducing the demand for specialist interventions
- Equipping the workforce to "think family" and intervene early
- Identifying children and young people at risk early

There are 16 Early Intervention projects and programmes in place across the city, all of which are now being evaluated.

Partnership working

Partnership working and **ownership by all relevant agencies and departments within the city** is a key principle underpinning the Early Intervention Programme. The Programme is supported by One Nottingham, the local strategic partnership and its partners, and is championed by the city council.

10. **Nottingham City** has developed an innovative Early Intervention approach over a number of years and was designated an Early Intervention City in April 2008.

Nottingham's Early Intervention model: by age, intervention and aim

11. Another set of initiatives, which I will explore in my second report, has taken into account the financial opportunities associated with Early Intervention. Birmingham City Council has used prudential borrowing of £40.7 million to support its programme of evidence-based Early Intervention programmes. On conservative assumptions, this investment is estimated to generate £101 million in future benefits. As evidence evolves about benefits, the money is returned for further investment in prevention and Early Intervention. Birmingham has begun to repay the loans used to establish its *Brighter Futures* programme.[4] Manchester is developing community budgets to support public sector reform, including cross-agency Early Intervention for highly vulnerable families. The budgets are replenished from the efficiencies created by implementing interventions that are proven to work. Cost-benefit analysis is used to ensure that investments are made by the agencies that are set to benefit. The end results are better support for children in their early years and for vulnerable families, reduced unemployment and breaking cycles of offending.

12. The charity Social Finance has been working with the Ministry of Justice to create financial instruments to bind relationships between funders and providers of services. The Peterborough Prison Pilot offers great potential as a model. Investors are rewarded when better outcomes – reduced recidivism – are translated into savings to the state through reduced casework for police, courts and probation and lower demand for prison places.

13. There is much promise in these and other local innovations in Early Intervention across the United Kingdom. However, our report also found weaknesses. First, even the most comprehensive of programmes, such as Birmingham, Nottingham and in Wales, are reaching just a small proportion of potential beneficiaries. Too many resources remain reserved for addressing problems that have already been allowed to escalate rather than intervening to resolve them earlier, when intervention could have been less intensive and therefore more economical. Hitherto, central government has been very good at letting wholly avoidable problems develop, ignoring them until they become chronic or publicly embarrassing and then hurriedly imposing a statutory duty on others to tackle them.

14. A second and analogous problem is that Early Intervention tends to be established on the edges of mainstream systems and supported by temporary public funding streams. It is not always given a stable footing.

15. Third, with notable exceptions including Birmingham, Brighton and Wales, the quality of evaluation is variable. Without adequate evaluation, good local practice is not identified and does not get recognised as excellent practice, like the evidence-based programmes described in the previous chapter.

16. A fourth and linked problem is poor communication about innovation across local settings. There is no common standard to determine what does and does not work. This makes it difficult for one locality to learn from another. It also promotes unhelpful competition, as several localities apply similar ideas with varying degrees of quality and no shared learning. Constant reinvention of the wheel is an expensive and wasteful activity, however satisfying to the inventors.

17. I have concluded, therefore, that much greater value should be accorded to local innovation, coupled with the support that will help to take good ideas to the highest standard and also allow respectful cessation of unsuccessful initiatives. I am struck by the automatic optimistic assumption that because Early Intervention is a rational strategy *every* local development in Early Intervention would be a success, although in every other walk of life people are prepared to accept that triumph is often the product of many defeats. Using the rhetoric and concept of Early Intervention is a necessary precondition for success. However, if we want to enhance local innovation to produce

national success we must have clear standards, better evaluation and improved dissemination of what works and what does not work.

Central government support

18. We have reached a moment where often brilliant local innovation on Early Intervention needs to link more effectively with excellent central government developments. The present government has made several welcome commitments to local communities, authorities and voluntary organisations to enhance Early Intervention. An additional 4,200 health visitors, combined with improved recruitment, retention and training, will better prepare and extend the reach of support for children in the first years of life. This investment reflects a recognition of health visitors' special ability to help children get a better start in life and to enable families to get better access other services.

19. This development goes hand in hand with the expansion of the evidence-based Early Intervention programme, the Family Nurse Partnership I described in the previous chapter. The government is committed to doubling the number of disadvantaged first-time, young mothers able to benefit from FNP at any one time by 2015.

20. The current national programme to provide free early education to 20,000 disadvantaged two year olds is to be extended to reach all disadvantaged two-year-olds (around 130,000) from 2013. Families will receive 15 hours of free, high quality early learning and care over 38 weeks of the year. Once their children reach three years of age they will be able to have the 15 hours of universal free early education that is available for every three- and four-year-old to support their development and readiness for school. While local authorities will decide with their communities on the right provision needed in each area, Sure Start children's centres will be asked to play a key role in encouraging the most disadvantaged two-year-olds to take up 15 hours of free early education each week. They will also be encouraged to identify and support those families in the greatest need. A fair and effective methodology for incentivising effectiveness through payment by results is also

being developed by the Department for Education. Other policy changes will help target these early years' resources towards the neediest families.

21. The Early Intervention Grant, worth about £2 billion by 2014, will promote cost-effective Early Intervention and prevention across England. The grant is intended to fund a wide range of Early Intervention strategies, which support vulnerable children and families, including those which tackle alcohol misuse, teenage pregnancy and anti-social behaviour and improve mental health support and crime prevention. It is also a tremendously important indicator that central government is taking Early Intervention seriously and for the first time has allocated a specific tranche of public expenditure towards it. .

22. The Pupil Premium, worth £2.5 billion by 2014-15, provides additional funding to schools for each deprived pupil in the country. The aim is to improve the attainment of students from deprived backgrounds by giving schools more funding to provide the right individual support for each pupil. I believe there is an opportunity for schools to consider the benefits of using some of this funding to build pupils' social and emotional competences as an important part of helping them to make the best of the learning opportunities open to them and, in the context of my review, develop skills that equip them for life.

23. The new Families with Multiple Problems Programme, announced by the Prime Minister on the 10 December 2010, is designed to turn around the lives of the most troubled families. With the programme providing new money for a number of areas through the Early Intervention Grant, it also provides a further opportunity to use proven Early Intervention approaches and programmes to help families with problems.

24. The government is also devolving control of public spending to 16 local areas via its Community Budgets initiative. The aim is to give local public service partnerships, such as health, justice, education, social work and other services (including those provided by voluntary and community organisations) more freedom to work together more effectively, help improve outcomes and reduce duplication and waste. The idea is to focus several funding streams, programmes

and efforts on locally agreed outcomes. These should include improved the social and emotional development of children. The intention is for Community Budgets to be available to all areas by 2013-14.

25. The recent review of the National Health Services for children and young people by Professor Sir Ian Kennedy stressed the importance of Early Intervention, including mental health, to improve lives in the long term, as well as improve cost effectiveness.[5]

26. Preventing problems before they become a crisis could potentially save **billions** of pounds for the NHS and the educational system. The government has pledged to support the extension of psychological therapies and to invest in mental health liaison and diversion services in police stations and courts.

27. I also hope that new policies and strategies being developed by the Home Office and the Ministry of Justice (MOJ), including the new crime strategy and the MOJ Green paper: Breaking the cycle: effective punishment, rehabilitation and sentencing of offenders, will enable criminal justice services to be key partners in Early Intervention at a local level and help embed a culture of Early Intervention in all public services.

The opportunity

28. I welcome the continued support for Early Intervention by the present government. A great opportunity now exists. Value can be added by connecting central and local initiatives in localities. I see additional health visitors, FNP and children's centres as a series of opportunities for a child born into a risky situation and a poor outcome. Instead of one-off programmes I propose a strategy for forging connections across government initiatives.

29. I propose, in a limited number of areas, an advantageous co-operation between government initiatives and local needs. In the past, local authorities and voluntary organisations have tended to grab as much of the central pie as they could. In an era when resources will be scarcer, greater benefit will be achieved by investing in initiatives best suited to local circumstances.

The proposal

30. I have concluded that much more could be made of existing local and national Early Intervention initiatives. In the previous chapter I reviewed the international literature, revealing in a short period of scrutiny over 80 evidence-based Early Intervention policies which could reliably improve the lives of children and families. From these I have selected 19 with a high degree of confidence over their expected returns as the best targets for new investment. The UK has high levels of innovation in this area but few of those innovations are rigorously evaluated or implemented more widely so that they become a routine part of local public services. In the UK, innovation tends to be piecemeal, and this is a great handicap when it comes to changing the balance between early and late intervention. For this reason I propose greater clarity around defining best programmes for the future.

31. I recommend that a small number of localities – in the form of a local authority, or a neighbourhood, or a series of neighbourhoods served by a several voluntary organisations – become focal points for innovation in Early Intervention. I call these Early Intervention Places. The precise selection procedure for Early Intervention Places can be decided by ministers in consultation with representatives of local government and the voluntary sector as well as the new Early Intervention Foundation I describe in the following chapter. My initial thinking was that about one in ten local authorities in England (15 in all) would need to show themselves best placed, in terms of both innovation and experience, to promote and implement Early Intervention locally.

32. In my consultations with local authorities and leaders of the voluntary sector for this Review, I informally asked if any would like to be "an Early Intervention Place". Even without full knowledge of the commitments involved, 26 came forward, such is the local demand for greater development in this important area. Those places that have agreed are listed at the end of this chapter.

33. These 26 are already discussing with me a number of practical issues including commitments:

- to adopt Early Intervention as a strategic priority and have secure buy-in with their partners to work together on Early Intervention 0-18, but with a particular focus on effective interventions in place pre-natal to age 3;

- to implement the Early Intervention approaches recommended in the Review;

- to commission work on the kind of programmes that meet the needs of their communities;

- to implement Early Intervention programmes with fidelity;

- to introduce best practice in monitoring and evaluating progress.

34. This preliminary discussion has already begun but it will not be highly productive unless the thinking of this Report is accepted by the government.

35. I would like all local areas to make the same commitments in due course and so the 15 areas selected as pioneers should not be seen as a definitive list. My proposal for an initial 15 simply recognises the importance of leading by example when trying to change collective behaviour.

36. I recognise that effecting change across the UK needs many local areas to reconsider their strategy and priorities. This is difficult to ask of local leaders at any time, but is particularly difficult in the current climate of significant funding pressures on local authorities and their partners. Although I am in touch with colleagues throughout the UK I will make no specific recommendations regarding Northern Ireland, Wales and Scotland until requested. However, it was obvious from the visits of the Review team and from all the evidence received that the devolved settlement has had a profoundly stimulating and creative impact on Early Intervention work, which I would hope to see replicated in a more empowered English local government.

37. I believe that the case for change has been made strongly in the previous chapters and that now is the time to seize this new way. With the support of local leaders, professionals and practitioners the change recommended by the Review is demanding but achievable.

38. I also believe that the support available to local areas to help with this change needs the same scale of improvement as that expected from local areas themselves and I address that issue in the next chapter.

39. I recommend that the 15 listed Places be given permission to find new ways to optimise local and national innovation. I believe that they could be helped, first by the Review team and then by the Early Intervention Foundation proposed in the next chapter, to develop in detail some of the many excellent ideas already included in this review, in particular to make use of the new financial flexibility offered by the Early Intervention Grant. In eight of the listed Places, local partners are also developing plans for Community Budgets to support families with multiple problems that have already emerged, but where broader early intervention practices and partnerships are likely to support and further enhance local activities. Therefore, I have provisionally agreed with the Secretary of State for Communities and Local Government that a number of these areas will be encouraged to use their interest in becoming an Early Intervention Place alongside their Community Budget plans to create an overlap between the two initiatives.

40. In addition, I have talked to the Department of Health and the Secretary of State for Justice. The Department of Health have offered to support an Early Intervention Place, which is focussed on health. This would make the best use of the new arrangements for public health to enhance Early Intervention at a local level . Positive discussions continue with Ministers at The Ministry of Justice , who agree that criminal justice services should be key partners in Early Intervention,.Here we could envisage support for a Place, with an emphasis on justice, to help demonstrate how criminal justice services can be key partners in Early Intervention. We are keen to develop this twinning of Places with other departments as our Places concept firms up.

41. I recommend that the Early Intervention Places be given permission to find new ways to optimise local and national innovation. I envisage that first the Review team and then the independent Foundation recommended in Chapter 8 could advise and agree with the Early Intervention Places the detail of some of the many

recommendations they made to us. Several of these stand out:

- allowing social enterprises that wish to provide Family Nurse Partnerships to use funds from local authority and health budgets because the benefits will be experienced by local authority social care services, through fewer children in foster care and in the child protection system;

- children's services working with health services and other partners sharing accountability for all of the resources going into a local area with all of the people living in that area, with the goal of using evidence-based Early Interventions to achieve better outcomes for children from existing or even reduced revenue streams;

- making available to private and public donors access to the emerging cost-benefit and benefit realisation technology being tested in Birmingham, Manchester and by Social Finance so that they can secure a return on their charitable investments;

- sharing costs of share set-up, implementation, monitoring and evaluation between voluntary and private providers of Early Intervention, which would allow them to improve the spread and the efficiency of services which have been jointly developed;

- enhancing the role of local partnerships as providers and funders for Early Intervention. If my recommendations are accepted I would look for some Early Intervention Places to be voluntary bodies or local strategic partnerships or similar forms of organisation.

42. It is self-evident that there is widespread and genuine excitement at local level in exploring some of these self-starting ideas if they can be released to do so. The Review recommends that the 15 local authorities (or neighbourhoods within those local authorities) who wish to are given the status of Early Intervention Places with permission to work together and with the foundation outlined in chapter 8.

43. The Review also supports exploring a changed relationship between central and local services (to allow for NHS inclusion) for Early Intervention. There has been a legacy of centrally-directed initiatives. There is an understandable desire to return power to local people, communities and agencies. However, many of the local people contributing to this report asked for guidance on issues such as evidence-based programmes, cost-benefit analysis, evaluation and independent financing. An effective relationship between central and local services should support local people in meeting local needs. For example, the Early Intervention Grant rightly respects local choice. But local people would value some guidance in the way of access to evidence on what works and how to realise the financial benefits of effective Early Intervention. I recommend that a new relationship between the 15 Early Intervention Places and central government is drawn up by the Review team, working closely with its local and central partners.

44. I would like the initial Early Intervention Places to become focal points for the other 127 local authorities in the UK. Better dissemination of innovation, success and failure will be invaluable to the natural spread of Early Intervention in the country. In place of directing localities to invest in Early Intervention, the objective will be to offer advice and to encourage early adopters of proven programmes, with demonstrated outcomes, cost-savings, high rates of return, consumer satisfaction and local innovation achieved in the Early Intervention Places.

45. At least 26 local authorities or consortia of local organisations, Including health services, have shown an interest in becoming an Early Intervention Place. My initial analysis shows that most have strong political commitment, a good track record of innovation, an understanding of the need to improve the evidence and use of new financial technologies, and the willingness to share results of their work, whether successful or not. These bodies are ready to move forward. They and the Review team will conclude these arrangements as soon as government accepts this recommendation

46. With proven cost-effective programmes available and a group of local organisations capable of choosing how to provide them, we need now to turn to the structure of support that both will require helping motivate and optimise their success- the Early Intervention Foundation.

Recommendations Chapter 7

47. I recommend that Early Intervention builds on the strength of its local base by establishing 15 local Early Intervention Places to spearhead its development. These should be run by local councils and the voluntary sector, who are already the main initiators and innovators of Early Intervention.

48. I recommend that where helpful the Places could voluntarily link to Government Departments where Early Intervention agendas overlap: positive preliminary discussions have already taken place with several Departments to explore this.

The Melton experience

Melton Borough Council has introduced an approach to work that has resulted in different thinking about how to solve problems, better working among agencies and tackling the root causes of issues and problems. In particular, it has sought to create a culture and a mindset of preventing failure by investing resources in Early Intervention.

It has moved away from traditional structures and introduced ones that cross administrative and departmental boundaries and that use collective knowledge to develop solutions to complex problems faced by people and places Within these structures staff have been placed in teams focussed on helping people to overcome disadvantage. This is a similar approach to Sure Start.

For example, Melton was worried by levels of crime and anti-social behaviour. It decided to gain a deep understanding of the individuals involved. It found:

- The cost of re-offending in Melton was calculated at £4.5 million a year.

- Young people were committing crime and acting anti-socially when they should have been in school. This was financially costly to the local community.

- Many families living in chaotic conditions, often in council properties, had children who were displaying worrying symptoms from a very young age.

- National research highlighted a single problem family could cost £250,00 – £350,000 a year.

- Detailed research into one of Melton's own problem families verified that different agencies were spending huge resources on families such as these without making things any better.

Offenders usually had similarity in their profiles, including low literacy and numerical skills, truanting or exclusion from school, mental and physical health problems and were more likely to be unemployed.

Melton wanted to focus on tackling the root causes, which meant going further back to ensure they were intervening at the earliest possible stage to prevent people from growing up in a way that was shown to almost inevitably lead to a life of crime and state dependency. Melton is already undertaking joined-up preventative work at the 22-weeks pregnancy stage, targeted at individuals and families deemed to be at high risk of experiencing poor outcomes.

26 areas have expressed an interest in becoming an Early Intervention Place

Birmingham
Blackpool
Bradford
Brighton and Hove
Croydon
East Sussex
Gateshead
Gloucestershire
Greater Manchester
Haringey
Harrow
Hertfordshire

Hull
Hounslow
Islington
Kingston Upon Thames
Lambeth
LancashireNottingham
Portsmouth
Somerset
Staffordshire
Stoke on Trent
Wakefield
Warrington
Westminster

The Highland experience

The streamlined rapid reaction model of Early Intervention being followed by Highland Region in Scotland has been running for ten years. The goal was to get things right for children the first time they were highlighted as being at risk, so they did not appear again later. This was judged to be more cost-effective than the previous local authority model where resource constraints were judged to prevent adequate intervention.

A number of principles were adopted to enable this shift to happen:

1) management of risk
2) integrated children's services and co-operatively working with other agencies
3) streamlining processes of response and reaction to risk
4) social Work structured differently (for example, a one social worker placed in each school)

To improve risk management, Highland Region re-examined its business processes, changed how agencies organised themselves to assess and manage risk, and introduced streamlined systems to improve reaction.

The introduction of integrated children's services began with studying the typical pathway of a child through its life and its potential contact with outside agencies. It was identified where in this pathway the earliest intervention could ensure the best long-term outcome and then developed practices that were more effective.

The core principle is that Early Intervention must be immediately to stop things escalating by convening a child's plan meeting attended by decision makers from each of the agencies with an interest in that family, the child and his or her parents. No matter who triggers this (school, health services, police) they must work in an integrated manner with other agencies and ensure fast response to need.

Results

Senior staff in Highland have highlighted that methods of working which allowed reaction at the critical point have led to much improved statistics for child protection; persistent offending; substance abuse; and improved outcomes for looked-after children. Social workers spend no more than 25 per cent of their time on bureaucracy and paperwork. In 2009 the general secretary of UNISON reported that the corresponding figure for England was 80 per cent.

Endnotes

1   Allen, G. and Duncan Smith, I. (2008) *Early Intervention: Good Parents, Great Kids, Better Citizens*. London: Centre for Social Justice and the Smith Institute

2   McDonald, L. (2010) Save the Children Launch with FAST UK (Families and Schools Together). Presentation at FAST Programme Launch, Save the Children Headquarters, Farringdon, London, 14th May.

3   For example, McDonald, L. and Frey, H. (1999) *Families and Schools Together: Building Relationships*. OJJDP Bulletin. Washington DC: US Department of Justice, Office of Justice Programs, Office of Juvenile Justice and Delinquency Prevention; McDonald, L., Moberg, P. D., Brown, R., Rodriguez-Espiricueta, I., Flores, N. I., Burke, M. P. and Coover, G. (2006) 'After-school multifamily groups: a randomized trial involving low-income, urban, Latino children', *Children and Schools 18*, 25-34; Kratochwill, T. R., McDonald, L., Levin, J. R., Scalia, P. A. and Coover, G. (2009) 'Families and schools together: an experimental study of multi-family support groups for children at risk', *Journal of School Psychology* 47, 245-265.

4   Birmingham City Council (2007) *The Brighter Futures Strategy*, Birmingham: Birmingham City Council; Birmingham City Council (2009) *A Brighter Future for Children and Young People: The Birmingham Strategy – The Story So Far*, Birmingham: Birmingham City Council.

5   Kennedy I., Getting it right for children and young people: overcoming cultural barriers into the NHS so as to meet their needs, 2010. www.dh.gov.uk/publications

Chapter 8
The Early Intervention Foundation:
Bringing Programmes and Resources to Places

"There is nothing more difficult to carry out, nor more doubtful of success, nor more dangerous to conduct than to initiate a new order of things. For the reformer has enemies in all who profit by the old order and only lukewarm defenders in all those who profit by the new order".

Machiavelli – The Prince

Introduction

1. Early Intervention must now take the next steps to turn concept into reality. It needs to grow from an activity in a few isolated areas to a universal one, with a strong base rooted in the philosophy of Early Intervention and enjoying the authority and respect to spread not only that philosophy but the best practice of Early Intervention. It will need the strongest political support from government and all parties, but will equally benefit from institutional arrangements that are independent from government. They will need to be credible with private and public investors, national and local public services, private and voluntary and community sector providers and bring together capital with programmes that are based on evidence.

2. However, the institutional arrangements I propose must be additions to mainstream funding, not replacements. However successful they prove, they can never provide the lion's share of resources required for successful Early Intervention: this will always rely on mainstream funding. An independent institution testing programmes, helping local councils and building coalitions with investors can only be a challenging and revitalising partner for the centre. Whitehall

will still control the policy of Early Intervention but if an additional source of advice, co-operation, methodology and even funding is available, the impact upon central provision will be healthy. This will have positive and invigorating effects upon centralised programmes, which will have much to gain as collaborators with independent partners.

3. I have made the case that too much money is spent once impairments to children's health and development have fully formed and become resistant to change. An overwhelming body of evidence now points towards the benefits of intervening early, before problems are out of hand. This means better intervention especially with those aged 0-3, but also with the 0-18s, especially in primary schools and early adolescence. At that stage, intervention should do more than react to the first manifestations of school failure and anti-social behaviour. It should also equip the 0-18s to make effective choices about their lives and, above all, to become good parents, thus breaking the transfer of dysfunction from one generation to the next.

4. The evidence base outlined in the first three chapters has long pointed towards the benefits of Early Intervention for child well-being and then for

fulfilling adult lives, particularly for society's most vulnerable. It is now supplemented by a strong economic case, outlined in chapter 4. Effective Early Intervention can produce significant financial returns, as the product of lower demands on local and national public services, both in childhood and adult life, and greater output and tax receipts from successful people of working age.

5. As chapter 6 records, there are now many hundreds of Early Intervention programmes and 19 of them have been demonstrated, on the highest scientific standards, to improve child outcomes. Many of these programmes are also supported by evidence about their economic worth. Emerging technology has brought nearer the day when one can make a precise calculation of the economic returns on effective Early Intervention programmes Preparation for that day must start immediately

6. The international evidence base is supplemented by strong national and local innovation in the United Kingdom. The last decade has seen a major, if uneven, advance in Early Intervention provision. This has been supported by all political parties and headlined by initiatives such as Sure Start children's centres and the Family Nurse Partnership. This has sponsored much local innovation, promoted by entrepreneurial organisations and individuals in communities that see the need for long-term change, including major initiatives highlighted throughout this report particularly in Birmingham, Nottingham, Northern Ireland and Wales. The present government has maintained support for Early Intervention and has shown itself open to adjusting the balance between centrally sponsored and locally sponsored innovation. This chapter supports the government's aim of allowing more local innovation to flourish, by proposing a new independent institution to act as its promoter, ally and champion.

7. However, the recent increase in early years' provision has not yet improved outcomes. The well-being of children in the UK continues to lag well behind that in other rich nations. In earlier chapters I charted some of the obstacles to Early Intervention. In total, Early Intervention remains a tiny part of total central and local government expenditure on children and, despite some notable

exceptions, it accounts for only a small part of total voluntary sector provision. In the UK, support for Early Intervention, while growing, is small scale. It is often dependent on ad hoc spending and not sustained by being in the mainstream of funding, and it is usually poorly evaluated. Almost all statutory provisions from Whitehall take the form of fire-fighting reactions to problems; few are about Early Intervention and pre-emption. Our political and official structures reinforce this tendency and it will take a brave decision to set out on a new path. Although our centralised nation leads most others in its ability to innovate within large-scale systems, its lack of sustained interest in rebalancing early and late intervention and the paucity of rigorous, high-quality evaluation means that few UK developments feature on international databases of good practice. Moreover, the lack of high-quality evaluation has made it unnecessarily difficult to estimate accurately the economic returns of Early Intervention. Time and again those who gave evidence to the Review commented that they promoted Early Intervention because it was right rather than because it had the central government endorsement and sustained resourcing.

8. The lack of clear standards of evidence ensures that he who shouts loudest gets the most business, not he who achieves most. There is little independent support for local innovators in the UK to help them to test their wares, or prove their impact, or demonstrate economic returns, or implement ideas more widely. There is poor dissemination of local successes and no attention to failure. Knowing what does not work is as important as what does, but learning from mistakes is not a part of new initiatives. Commissioners of programmes have no source of independent advice on what works, for whom, when and why, and this makes it difficult for them to have confidence in new approaches.. As yet, only a handful of councils are using information which offers cost-benefit analysis to select between competing investment options, a particular handicap to Early Intervention programmes that produce the greatest returns. When central and local government does invest in proven approaches, there can be a lackadaisical approach to fidelity– staying true to

the programme- meaning that intended effects are often lost.

9. I make three broad recommendations in response to the lack of progress. First, I believe that proven Early Intervention models such as those described in Chapter 6 should become more available in UK. I recommend that alongside this development greater support should be given to local innovators to reach higher standards of evidence, which will help to get more UK models onto international databases of proven practice.

10. Second, I recommend the creation of Early Intervention Places to make a coherent start on Early Intervention, giving permission for 15 localities to make the most of central and local initiatives. This would involve the use of central government initiatives in the 15 sites, greater flexibility for those in the Places to innovate and evaluate, and better dissemination support so that local areas can learn from each other. At the heart of these recommendations is a commitment to localism, to support local innovation, and for central government to be the national advocate, encouraging and enabling local people rather than controlling their activities. However, my Review team also heard many calls from local people and agencies for high-quality central advice to avoid expensive replication of provision. Localities do need additional support to help them make optimal decisions from the many options now available to them. There is clearly a thirst for such an alternative or additional offer. The following quotations are typical of the comments made by contributors to the evidence sessions I held for the review:

"We need help to explain the importance of Early Intervention. It isn't recognised by all the right people locally, including political leaders";

"There are problems with the way Early Intervention initiatives or programmes are implemented. All of the good ideas and enthusiasm at the beginning of a project needs to be sustained as it is taken to scale. We have a poor track record in this";

"Guidance on which programmes are going to give us the best result given our local needs would be welcome. As commissioners we

are bombarded with directives from central government and requests for business from private and voluntary organisations. More support to make better decisions would help us a lot";

"It is difficult to join up services that are funded through different government funding streams, for example health and education."

11. To meet these frequent comments from contributors, my third broad recommendation is to establish an Early Intervention Foundation to support local people, communities and agencies, with initial emphasis on the 15 Early Intervention Places. It would also tie in to the potential of raising capital from private and other investors, which I will examine further in my second report. An additional responsibility of the Foundation would be to help local agencies make the best use of central government initiatives. This chapter sets out the potential contribution of the foundation. It also makes suggestions about its governance.

The objective

12. I recommend that the foundation be charged with establishing demonstrable improvements in the social and emotional bedrock of children in the 15 Early Intervention Places. In addition, it should be able to sell its services to the many other local authorities who are already showing an interest in the proposal. I believe that pump-priming funding could be sought potentially from local government, foundations and private investors. Central government would provide the strongest possible political support (always on an all-party basis) but initial central government financial help, while always welcome, may not be essential. Indeed, there is a strong argument that it will be much easier for the Foundation to attract private and non-governmental investment capital if it is seen to be independent (rather than an arm) of central government. I describe below how this could work. My aspiration aim is for the Early Intervention Foundation to become self-funding as quickly as possible. Part 2 of my review will consider the appropriate models for achieving this.

13. Given the current financial climate, I recognise that it would be very difficult, if not impossible, for such a venture to be taken on by government,

although even in better economic times there are several compelling reasons to keep it independent. There are a number of potential non-government investors. While the funding and finance options explored in my second report will look at continuing investment, initial capital from local government, philanthropists and social enterprises is already a possibility. Many investors are keen to do something positive for society and support a foundation which could help them to develop the people and workforce of the future.

14. The Review team will therefore aim to build on the existing momentum in seeking private and non-governmental investment. My second Report will define more precisely the scope of the Foundation, set out the best non-government options for its initial funding and identify potential new sources of future investment.

Purpose and general functions of the Foundation

15. The Foundation would have the following purpose and general functions:

- **Leadership and motivation**

  It would work across all sectors and throughout the UK to champion the importance and impact of Early Intervention and to promote the need for sustainable policies, strategies and arrangements for Early Intervention;

- **Strategies**

  It would expand and improve the provision of Early Intervention across the UK;

- **Locally focussed**

  It would work with local authorities, other local services and their partners to support the continuing development of the evidence for Early Intervention set out in this review;

  It would maintain and enhance a database of cost-effective local programmes;

  It would develop robust outcomes monitoring and evaluation arrangements on behalf of localities in order to provide independent reassurance to government and investors in Early Intervention that outcomes have been achieved and financial savings realised;

- **Funding**

  It would encourage new investment to provide of Early Intervention;

  It would act as a trusted source of information for philanthropists wishing to provide funding in this area;

  It would actively market effective Early Intervention policies to local authorities and funders.

Benefits to Local Areas

16. There are several areas of advice and support that could help to optimise Early Intervention in local areas, many of which were highlighted in the responses to the Review. These areas are set out below, and indicate where the Foundation could best offer support to those providing Early Intervention:

a. *Reliable evidence on the Early Intervention policies and programmes which are most likely to improve outcomes for children and young people and produce economic savings.* This includes defining and communicating clear standards of evidence, with robust methodologies for measuring the cost-benefit analysis and effectiveness of programmes. The Foundation could maintain and develop databases and directories of effective programmes, policies, relevant research and evaluation as a core part of its library of evidence. The Foundation would be responsible for disseminating evidence to providers.

I have drawn heavily in the earlier sections of this report on standards of evidence developed by the Greater London Authority in collaboration with the Social Research Unit at Dartington and later validated by an international panel of experts. I recommend that the Foundation, when established, should undertake further independent consultation on these and other viable options, and make any necessary alterations before publishing a set of national standards to guide future investment decisions.

I also drew on a database of effective Early Intervention policies and programmes being prepared by the Institute of Effective Education at York, the Blueprints for Violence Prevention Group at the University of Colorado in Boulder, Missouri, USA, the Social Research Unit at Dartington, and the Social Development Research Group at the University of Washington. I recommend that the Foundation supports a UK panel of independent experts to validate a comprehensive list of effective policies and programmes and update it regularly, in consultation with an appropriate international development team.

The Foundation should draw on existing expertise in the evaluation of programmes, such as the Centre for Evidence-Based Intervention at Oxford University and the National Academy for Parenting Research at King's College London. Both include researchers with first-hand expertise in undertaking high quality evaluations, and staff with experience as practitioners. NAPR has developed the commissioning toolkit to help commissioners choose effective parenting programmes including those developed by the voluntary sector.

Local authorities such as Birmingham, Manchester and the Greater London Authority are funding the Social Research Unit at Dartington to translate an econometric model developed by the Washington State Institute for Public Policy for use in the UK. The product of this work will be freely available "open source" software that can be used by public and private sector investors to calculate the risks and benefits of competing investment options. I recommend that the Foundation should consider relevant methodologies such as this, which could be made available to local providers such as the Early Intervention Places identified earlier. The Foundation should provide a hub of expertise for this type of methodology.

I recommend that that the foundation provides publications, tools and advice aimed at changing the balance between UK and non-UK contributions to the database of proven Early Intervention policies and practices. the Foundation should also be charged with improving the quality of dissemination in the field of Early Intervention.

b. *Implementation of programmes*, including access to relevant tools, and development of necessary skills to help local providers provide Early Intervention programmes. The problem of poor fidelity of implementation is now well understood by local agencies and central government, but few of the tools available to address this issue are either known or used. I recommend that the Foundation bring together the manuals, training and coaching materials required to get the best from evidence-based Early Intervention programmes and find efficient mechanisms to make them available to the purchasers of these interventions including the Early Intervention Places. Part of this task will involve working with programme developers and connecting them to local commissioners. This would include supporting local areas to implement models in a consistent manner, replicating and adhering to the original model. The Foundation could also support the wider use of promising initiatives, helping to turn them into models, which are evaluated and based on evidence. It could also advise on the professional development of the Early Intervention workforce and how its members acquire the skills which they need. Part of the role of the Foundation would be to ensure consistent methodologies (including application of consistent measures of well-being).

c. *Tools to estimate need and demand.* My colleague Rt Hon Frank Field MP has recommended the development of a measure of the well-being of children in the first five years of life, on the basis that it is difficult to recover from developmental deficits at this stage of life.[1] I wholeheartedly support this recommendation. My Review team encountered many tools that not only measure well-being in the early years but also at later stages of development. Unfortunately, good measures may be crowded out by the volume of other information demanded of local authorities, and from private and public providers. I recommend that the Foundation be charged with taking an independent view on the minimum data requirements on local agencies and to switch the emphasis from central monitoring of local action to information that will help local agencies make optimaldecisions about whom to help, when and how. The quality of evaluation of Early Intervention in the UK has fallen behind international standards. New technology has emerged that allows precise estimates of the impact of policies and programmes on local children, producing the information necessary to calculate costs and benefits. I recommend that the Foundation support the wider implementation of these replication evaluation methods in those 15 Early Intervention Places that wish it.

d. *Facilitating greater investment in evidence-based Early Intervention, including attracting private sector investors.* The Foundation could help to bring together investors with robust Early Intervention programmes that require additional funding.

The Foundation could help support investment in its role as an advocate for Early Intervention, helping to demonstrate the benefits of the approach to investors. It could operate as an intermediary between central government, local government and funders and Early Intervention programmes, helping to provide the evidence of what should best be done at local level, and promoting more effective co-ordination of resources. It could encourage investment, for instance by helping to spread risk across a wide range of programmes through a more co-ordinated approach, direct resources to approved schemes, and manage the interface between investors and commissioners and providers. This will be considered in more detail in Part 2 of my Review.

Although its financial role will be a primary focus of the Foundation, its structure should prevent any possible conflict of interest between this and its role of evaluation. That means considering how best to separate decisions on the effectiveness of specific programmes from decisions on finance. Part 2 of the review will also need to explore how the finance arm of the foundation should best be structured to comply with state aid, accounting, regulatory and other relevant considerations.

e. *Greater co-ordination and brokering of improved working across organisations.* The Foundation could help to bring together providers of Early Intervention, helping to overcome organisation boundaries through a shared purpose. Through greater co-ordination, the Foundation could help to stimulate a growing market of providers. It could also help to oversee and advise on relevant links with other parts of the system, including programmes for adults.

Functions

17. As I stated earlier the Foundation will provide leadership and motivation. It does not need to undertake all the activities required for Early Intervention. If there is an existing institution which has proved its ability to meet the expectations of the Foundation and the needs of stakeholders, it may choose to continue to commission activities from that institution. For example, there are a number of organisations which carry out some activities in Early Intervention where I expect the Foundation to lead. They include the Centre for Excellence and Outcomes in Children and Young People Services, National Institute for Health and Clinical Excellence, the Social Care Institute for Excellence and (for the time being) the Children's Workforce Development Council although all of these organisations have a much broader remit than Early Intervention. The Foundation would work with these organisations to either ensure appropriate priority is given to early intervention in their work or commission activities from them where they were best placed to provide them. Similarly, when gaps are identified the Foundation may choose to seek other providers of the services needed when that is the most effective option. This approach should help the Foundation to be relevant to all parts of the UK and to all stakeholders, and allow existing expertise and experience to be maintained and improved. To give one example, central government and all commissioners of public services are increasingly looking at payment by results as a model for contracts. The key to success on these contracts, whether they are just outcome contracts funded in a traditional manner or social impact contracts , funded by the issuing of a bond or other financial product, is what the contract will provide including

the clear identification of the outcomes and results to be achieved that will trigger payment. Equally important, will be the measurement of those outcomes. It has been suggested during our Review[2] that an important role for an independent foundation could be to provide the honest broker role for commissioners, providers and investors in relation to both defining and measuring outcomes across the public sector. (Additional support for this view came from Clay Yaeger TITLE who spoke to the Review in December 2010. He has provided such measurement and outcomes from the private sector in several parts of North America, including Pennsylvania and Florida.) This would allow the Foundation to develop its role as a centre of expertise and good practice in the fields of Early Intervention and outcome-based projects.

Governance

18. Governance arrangements should reflect the requirements of funders and other stakeholders and, as I have already suggested, it will need to ensure that there is effective separation between the financial and other arms of the Foundation, to avoid any conflict of interest.

19. I believe that sectors outside central government are best placed to create the Foundation in a short time, ideally in the form of a social enterprise. Much of the technology provided by the Foundation could be made available to other bodies within the UK but the Foundation would remain responsible for using this technology to generate economic returns for the 15 Early Intervention Places and private investors.

20. A board of directors would include representation from investors, local users and independent experts. I recommend that government be given an observer role.

Funding

21. I strongly believe that the Foundation should be independent of government and self-funding. Given the rapidly changing economic context in which local agencies are operating, I would like it to be operational this year in order to provide at least some of its services to the Early Intervention

Places and other investors by the summer of 2011. I anticipate a small, efficient organisation that finances itself from demand for its services.

22. A detailed business plan would be drawn up by the partners that form the independent foundation. In addition, the Foundation would be encouraged to seek other finance from national funders that will respect its independent status.

23. I have begun to explore private and philanthropic sources to pump-prime the new enterprise and a number of significant individuals and organisations have already welcomed the progress made so far.

Summary

24. The application of Early Intervention policies in our country is patchy in geography and uneven in quality. They are not evaluated to any common standards and little effort is made to identify the policies which work best, to learn from success and failure, or to disseminate best practice. I believe that the Early Intervention Foundation, as described above, could remedy all of these problems. I believe that its establishment is fundamental to the success of Early Intervention programmes and their expansion. It could provide the rigour and expertise which could inform existing policy, encourage innovation and entice private as well as public investors to provide sustainable funding for the right Early Intervention programmes.

25. The creation of such a Foundation requires foresight and boldness from the government. There will be many vested interests keen to keep the status quo. However, the conjunction of factors – a new government, economic restraint, a financial community eager to make a contribution, a burst of energy from localism and the willingness of a group of local authorities and entrepreneurs willing to make it happen – offer the perfect moment to make the significant change that Early Intervention needs. I recommend the creation of a shadow Early Intervention Foundation to take these proposals to fruition.

Recommendations-Chapter 8

26. I recommend the establishment of an independent Early Intervention Foundation to support local people, communities and agencies, with initial emphasis on the 15 Early Intervention Places.

27. I recommend that the Foundation should be led and funded by non-central government sources, including local government, ethical and philanthropic trusts, foundations and charities as well as private investors. There is already considerable interest in this. The government should champion and encourage this concept. Whitehall should neither control nor isolate the Foundation but welcome it and engage with it as a source of complementary activity and advice.

28. I recommend that the Foundation be given the following roles: to lead and motivate the expansion of Early Intervention; to evaluate Early Intervention policies based on a rigorous methodology and a strong evidence base, and encourage others to do the same; to advise the 15 Places and other local councils and organisations; and to develop the capacity to attract private and public investment to Early Intervention.

29. 34. I recommend the immediate creation of a 'shadow' Early Intervention Foundation [including as members those quoted in annex one if they are willing] be set up forthwith to bring these proposals to fruition.

Endnotes

1   Field, F (2010), *Independent Review on Poverty and Life Chances*

2   Charlesworth, I, *Social Investment Ltd*

Chapter 9
Making it Happen:
Strong Leadership across the Parties

I believe that this report has demonstrated a compelling case for a re-balancing of the present expensive and largely ineffective system of late intervention towards Early Intervention, which offers a real prospect of lasting success and savings. The current imbalance is so great that almost certainly this transition can be achieved only in incremental stages. Nonetheless, it will still entail a significant cultural change. *That cannot be achieved by purely administrative means. It requires clear vision and committed leadership across the political class. Strong leadership at a national and local level is the single most critical factor in extending Early Intervention to all those that would benefit. I hope this leadership will be most obviously demonstrated by the response to the recommendations of this report.*

1. At a national level, such leadership must be based on increasing recognition of the benefits across generations and cost-effectiveness of Early Intervention, building on the steps already taken by this government and its predecessor. All governments henceforward need to make sure that the appropriate policies and incentives are in place to help local political or community leaders to implement and maintain sustainable Early Intervention strategies and programmes for their communities.

2. As I have argued repeatedly, change to affect different generations has to span many electoral cycles and cannot be the property of any one political party. This will require ongoing cross--party support. When Iain Duncan Smith and I published our book in 2008[1] all of the then leaders of the major UK parties gave public support to its vision of Early Intervention. I am grateful that the same is true for this report. Even in the UK's fevered political and media environment a space exists for politicians of all parties to commit themselves to a common goal. If they cannot do this when the goal is the well-being of our children, what hope is there for our political system?

Recommendations

3. I Even before the publication of this Review I had written to all party leaders to ask that they continue to work together on Early Intervention policies in the future in a way which builds on the recommendations of this Review.

Clear political responsibility

4. Ministers throughout government have been encouraging and positive as our work has progressed. Our ultimate line of account is to the Cabinet Social Justice Committee. This has worked well for our report. However, if this more nimble and swift Early Intervention strategy is to be implemented it needs an equally adept response from government. The traditional remedy for all policy ills is to propose a new minister for the subject. I do not suggest that. The Prime Minister is best placed to make that judgement. The vital task is to ensure effective co-ordination between ministers and get departments to operate outside their siloes. That is the only hope of success for a cross-cutting policy such as Early Intervention. It is crucial to get the machinery right, especially when investments by one department improve the outcomes of other departments. There are a plethora of reviews, officials committees in and around this field that not only need co-ordination but need ownership, energy and direction from the top. Early Intervention will depend on establishing lines of accountability which are well-designed and sustainable. One responsible minister is a possibility, but so, too, is a triumvirate of Cabinet Office, Education and Health ministers, and other forms of responsibility and accountability for Early Intervention are imaginable and defensible.

5. From my perspective the most obvious solution would be for the Deputy Prime Minister, who is already taking a lead on social mobility, to have the role of motivating the government-wide effort on Early Intervention through the Cabinet Office. The key point is to resolve this issue in one way or another at the outset. That would be a tremendously encouraging signal for everyone who wants to get on with the essential job of implementing Early Intervention.

I recommend that the Cabinet Social Justice Committee resolves the issue of future ownership of Early Intervention policy immediately on presentation of this Review.

A new relationship between Whitehall and local providers

6. The officials of our strongly centralised state in Whitehall also have a key role to play, beyond working more fluently across departmental borders. They are sometimes perceived on the ground –rightly or wrongly – as having over-prescribed and over-targeted local activity. With Early Intervention, they now have a unique opportunity to recognise that their best contribution is to be seen to be supporting ideas and actions outside of their control. Early Intervention goes with the flow of the present government's strategy of decentralisation and localism, and my main recommendations require local government and voluntary sector ownership. The large departments will still command 99 per cent of budget and expenditure on the issues addressed by Early Intervention and they can only gain from the external policy evaluation and intellectual challenge on from the proposed independent Early Intervention Foundation. In administrative terms, Whitehall is the equivalent of Tesco's: it will not be harmed by planning permission for the Foundation's corner shop. Through the course of my Review I have met many Permanent Secretaries and Directors-General to discuss Early Intervention and am encouraged by their genuine desire to move it forward. It leads me to believe that they will take an imaginative and sympathetic approach to establishing the right relationships with local government, the voluntary sector, and the Early Intervention Foundation.

As soon as ministers resolve their approach, I recommend that the commitment across government to Early Intervention should be given the strongest and most active leadership by the Permanent Secretaries Committee especially on how to join up departmental thinking and delivery on Early Intervention, and in particular how to get buy-in from local authorities.

Local providers: accountability and advice

7. Local government elected leaders and senior officials already have a clear responsibility, with transparent accountability, for improving outcomes for children and young people.

I believe that they should enhance this by measuring their progress against the indicators recommended in the Review of the readiness of children and young people for school, work and life. However, the imposition of some top-down local Early Intervention plan should be resisted. It is strategically important that the next steps for Early Intervention should be taken by a coalition of the willing, enthusiasts who want to pursue it because they see the long- term benefits. Of course, many local councils and voluntary organisations want to learn from the best, perhaps by forming their own local action plan, but I do not believe that central government is the best location for that advice. Instead, I believe that they will be better served by independent advice from the sources I propose in this Review, especially the Early Intervention Foundation.

8. I recommend that the successful interaction with local government, begun by the Review, should be continued and developed, especially by giving local government a leading role in the Early Intervention Foundation.

Momentum

9. 5 It is not normal for policy reviews to address the issue of momentum. But every political reader of this Review will understand why I do so now. There are brief windows in political life when a big idea has the chance to capture the imagination and support of the general public and the official machine. At such times, that big idea needs momentum, not delay. Early Intervention is now in that moment. In the few brief weeks I have had to conduct this Review it has become evident to me that political and financial circumstances have converged to create a perfect opportunity to make a qualitative leap forward for Early Intervention. *In order to capture that opportunity and generate real momentum for Early Intervention I have deliberately made recommendations which require no new primary legislation and no additional public expenditure.* If the government supports my proposals – and has the political will to step back and give greater freedom to local providers – they could be implemented swiftly.

10. Few people, if any, would wish to park these proposals –for to do so would waste a unique opportunity – and it is necessary to move forward smartly..For this purpose, assuming that my key proposals in chapters 6, 7 and 8 are agreed by the Cabinet Social Justice Committee, there needs to be a transition team to effect their implementation. This team would be based around the Review team but be able to draw on whatever specialist help is required. Since my key proposals call for action outside Whitehall I believe that such a transition team should have a majority of non-governmental –and potential Early Intervention Foundation – members.

I recommend that a transition team be established to implement the key recommendations accepted by the cabinet committee.

Endnotes

1   Allen, G. and Duncan Smith, I. (2008) *Early Intervention:
    Good Parents, Great Kids, Better Citizens*. London: Centre
    for Social Justice and the Smith Institute.

Chapter 10
Financing Early Intervention

1. The completion of this first report is not the end of the story. Not only must it be acted upon, but if its key recommendations are accepted they will need to be supported by greater finance for Early Intervention. That is why the Review team is staying together and is already preparing its second report on Early Intervention funding and finance. I have already set out my belief that the expansion of Early Intervention can be better achieved if championed by a new Early Intervention Foundation. In my view, this could be largely achieved through non-government sources, although the government would always be welcome as an investor. The next task is to examine how we can achieve this and to investigate the full range of financial mechanisms that could attract external investment. This part of the Review will have the help of the Treasury and the expert advice of the City and financial community. In addition, there are many ethical and philanthropic institutions that have already made pertinent contributions. Many readers of this report are already working with the Review team, but it still welcomes ideas and contributions from all sources, and can be contacted at [Insert generic email address] or [insert address for written submissions]

2. I hope that this report has established its central case: there is massive saving to be made from helping babies, children and young people make the best of themselves rather than cost society and the taxpayer billions of pounds for want of a modest investment. The next task is to discover the best way to use that massive potential saving to drive up-front investment in Early Intervention policies. We need to be able to measure it, put a price on it, and ring-fence it so that the gain can be repaid to public and private investors, and if we can achieve this, many of those investors would almost certainly reinvest some or all of their gain in yet more Early Intervention.

3. This report has already shown that there is a set of strong programmes, with compelling evidence of effectiveness, which would be able to produce returns and develop confidence in Early Intervention investments. The broad-based independent foundation recommended in Chapter 8 would be able to advise and to help develop Early Intervention. There is no shortage of potential instruments to finance Early Intervention, including local council and other bonds, equity-based products, payment-by-results organisations and High Street retail products. The Review team will examine them all, and consider how the proposed Foundation could best support them.

4. That work starts in earnest today: I hope that all readers will help to make it a success.

Annex A
What they say about Early Intervention

"Local government will be delighted if a locally-driven Institution of the type floated in the Allen Report is given the job of breaking through on Early Intervention. Rigorous evidence based policies and strong methodologies, faithfully implemented are the key to combining localised decision making with the most effective programmes around. At a time of scarce public resources it's even more important that we implement evidenced based programmes proved to work and tackle the causes of social problems rather than always be forced to deal with their consequences.

"I would urge government to look further into the Allen Report and enable us to build an independent centre to take this work forward."

Stephen Hughes
Chief Executive Birmingham City Council

"The Big Lottery Fund shares Graham Allen's ambition for excellent early intervention to improve outcomes for children and families. Knowing what works, funding it effectively, and influencing and supporting practitioners on the ground, are all crucial components for success.

"As a funder, BIG supports many civil society organisations that reach out to and deliver services for families, who could benefit from opportunities for their practice to be shared more widely and validated, as well as opportunities to learn from best practice elsewhere. We therefore look forward to studying the proposals that emerge from Graham Allen's review and considering how best we as a funder can support early intervention that works."

Sir Peter Wanless, chief executive, The Big Lottery

"If Early Intervention is to go to the next level, the Private Equity Foundation believes that an institution independent of central government which can identify the best proven interventions, facilitate their delivery by local providers and attract private funders by demonstrating the quality, effectiveness and results of these programmes and policies would be critical. We would be keen to play our part in transforming the ideas in the first Allen report into action and contributing ideas to the second report on different forms of non-government financing of Early Intervention."

Charlie Green, Trustee, Private Equity Foundation

"It's already an exciting time for City involvement in Early Intervention and similar programmes The Allen review proposals open up more possibilities to develop this relationship even further."

Jim O'Neil Chair. Goldman Sachs Asset Management

"I welcome the idea of the development of an independent intermediary institution linking the communities of finance, local government and evidence-based early intervention policies, whether built on and with existing intermediaries or established separately if necessary. I would be very happy to be involved in discussions in this area should government give approval in principle to the idea going ahead, given its alignment with our focus on social investment in the development of the Big Society."

Lord Wei, government adviser on the Big Society

"The Allen Report opens up the possibility for City Investment schemes to flow into tried and tested Early Intervention programmes forging the link between attractive rates of return for investors and serious benefits for individuals and their families. We need to make the step up from individual philanthropy to sustained private income streams. An Early Intervention Foundation could be the vehicle to make this happen and I hope Government will allow those who wish to take this further, to do so."

Chris Robinson, Chief Executive, The Mayor's Fund for London

"An independent Foundation separate from central government, created and led by local councils, private investment and charitable and ethical partners, could impartially evaluate and make freely available the most cost-effective early intervention policies, help put them into practise and explore new resources from non government funding. Graham's Review recommendations demand a serious appraisal and an urgent response."

Sir Howard Bernstein, Chief Executive, Manchester City Council

"Early Intervention must take the next steps forward. We would consider working with others to help get an institution off the ground that could act as a broker between the different interests in early intervention, commissioners, investors and deliverers to develop policies and models of intervention, as well as defining and measuring outcomes. Good work is being done in this area by government and others. It now needs to be given additional clout and an extra dimension."

Ian Charlesworth, Commercial Director, The Social Investment Business

"The police service has much to gain from capable parenting. Raising socially and emotionally capable babies, children and young people is important, since this will inevitably mean fewer offenders in later life. Should an Early Intervention Foundation be agreed by the Government we would want to be closely involved with local authority and other partners to help maximise its value."

Ian McPherson QPM, Assistant Commissioner, Metropolitan Police

Annex B
Programmes and how they were selected

The process by which evidence-based interventions were selected, and allocated to the three levels, is set out in the flowchart below

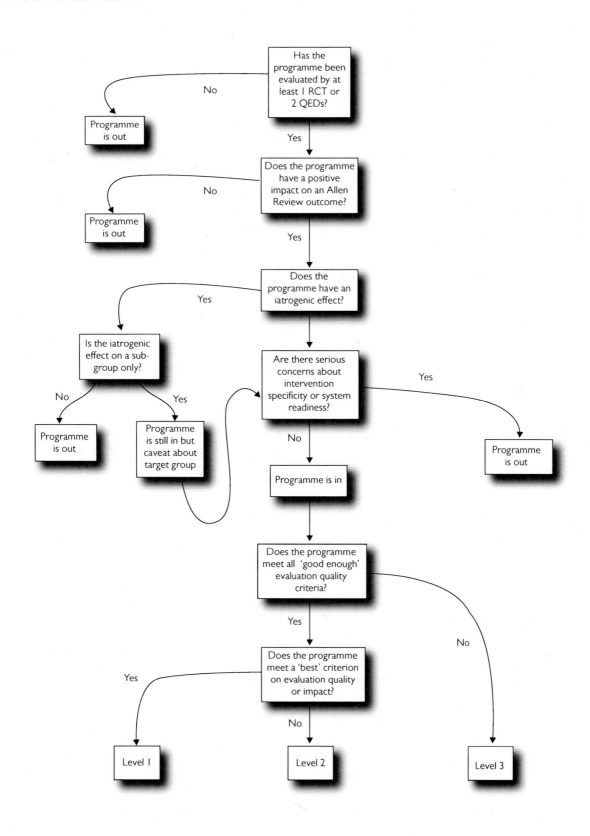

The three levels of evidence are defined as follows, starting with the highest standard:

Level 1

All of the level 2 criteria must apply plus:

Programme gets a 'best' on evaluation quality and/or impact criteria. In the case of Evaluation quality this means that any of the 'best' criteria must apply, while in the case of Impact both of the 'best' criteria must apply

Level 2

All of the level 3 criteria must apply plus:

Programme meets all evaluation quality criteria

Level 3

All of the following must apply:

Programme has 1 Randomised Controlled Trial (RCT) or 2 Quasi-Experimental Designs (QED)

Programme has a positive impact on an Allen Review outcome

Programme has no iatrogenic effect

There are no obvious concerns about intervention specificity or system readiness

The criteria and guidance used to inform this work are listed in the Appendix B of this Report. They are based on the standards developed by The Social Research Unit for the Greater London Authority's Project Oracle. These were further developed with the help of leading experts in the field of Early Intervention at the the Annie E. Casey Foundation, the Social Development Research Group at the University of Washington and the Blueprints for Violence Prevention Group in the United States as well as the Institute for Effective Education in the UK.

The institutions and individuals involved in review of the criteria, and coding of programmes against these standards, is listed below.

The panel used to inform selection

Lead individuals

Delbert Elliott
(University of Colorado, Boulder, and Developer of the Blueprints for Violence Prevention database)

David Hawkins
(Social Development Research Group, University of Washington, US, and Developer of the Prevention Strategies Guide that is part of Communities that Care)

Michael Little
(The Social Research Unit, Dartington, UK)

Kristen Moore
(Child Trends, Washington, US, and Developer of the LINKS database)

Robert Slavin
(Success for All, Johns Hopkins University, US, and Developer of the Best Evidence Encyclopaedia)

Reviewers

Nick Axford
Gretchen Bjornstad
Frances Kemp
Michaela Santen
(The Social Research Unit, Dartington, UK)

Nicole Eisenberg
Andrew Woolley
(Social Development Research Group, University of Washington, US)

Abigail Fagan
(University of North Carolina, US)

Tawana Bandy
Jordan Khan
Mary Terzian
(Child Trends, US)

Bette Chambers
(Success for All, US)

Selected Programmes by level

The following programmes have been assigned to levels 1, 2 or 3 based on the process described above. Further summaries of programmes, their target group and the broad outcomes areas are included below.

Level 1 (19 interventions)

– Curiosity Corner (As part of Success for All)
– Early Literacy and Learning
– Functional Family Therapy (FFT)
– Incredible Years
– Let's Begin with the Letter People
– Life Skills Training (LST)
– Lion's Quest Skills for Adolescence
– Multisystemic Therapy (MST)
– Multidimensional Treatment Foster care (MTFC)
– Nurse Family Partnership (NFP)
– Parent Child Home Programme
– PATHS
– Project TND
– Reading Recovery
– Ready, Set, Leap!
– Safe Dates
– Safer Choices
– STARS for Families
– Success for All

Level 2 (3 interventions)

– Bright Beginnings
– Parent Child Interaction Therapy (PCIT)
– Schools and Families Together (SAFE Children)

Level 3 (50 interventions)

– Adolescents Coping with Depression
– Adolescent Transitions Program
– All Stars
– Al's Pals
– Brain Power
– Breakthrough to Literacy
– Brief Strategic Family Therapy

– Bright Bodies
– Career Beginnings
– Caring Schools Communities
– Carrera Pregnancy Prevention [effect on girls only][1]
– CASASTART
– CATCH
– Community Mothers
– Cooperative Integrated Reading and Composition
– Coping Power
– Dare to be You
– Direct Instruction
– Even Start
– First Step to Success
– Good Behavior Game
– Guiding Good Choices
– Healthy Families America
– Healthy Families New York
– High/Scope Perry Pre-School
– Homebuilders
– I Can Problem Solve
– Olweus Bullying Program
– PALS
– Parenting Wisely
– Parents as Teachers
– Planet Health
– Positive Action
– Power Teaching Mathematics
– Power Teaching Mathematics (STAD)
– Project SPARK
– Quick Reads
– Reducing the Risk
– Read 180
– Roots of Empathy
– Shapedown
– Stop Now and Plan (SNAP)
– TAI Math
– Targeted Reading Intervention

– Teen Outreach

– The Reading Edge

– Together Learning Choices (TLC)

– Triple P

– Varying Maternal Involvement in a Weight Loss Program

– Youth AIDS Prevention Project

Selected Programs by developmental stage and target group

The table below shows where these programmes fit in terms of developmental stage they apply to (rows) and target group (columns).

Some programs cut across different developmental stages (indicated by brackets). For example, Al's Pals appears in 'Conception to school/ Interventions for all children' but also in 'Primary school/Interventions for all children'.

	Interventions for all children	Interventions for children in need
Conception to school	Al's Pals Breakthrough to Literacy Bright Beginnings Curiosity Corner I Can Problem Solve Incredible Years Let's Begin with the Letter People Parents as Teachers Ready, Set, Leap! Success for All Triple P	Brief Strategic Family Therapy Community Mothers Dare To Be You Early Literacy and Learning[2] Even Start[3] Healthy Families America Healthy Families New York High/Scope Perry Pre-School (Incredible Years) Multidimensional Treatment Foster Care (MTFC) Nurse Family Partnership Parent-Child Home Program[4] Parent-Child Interaction Therapy (PCIT) (Triple P)

	Interventions for all children	Interventions for children in need
Primary school years	(Al's Pals)	(Brief Strategic Family Therapy)
	Brain Power	Bright Bodies
	(Breakthrough to Literacy)	Coping Power
	Caring Schools Communities	(Even Start)
	CASASTART	First Step to Success
	CATCH	Homebuilders
	Cooperative Integrated Reading and Composition	(Incredible Years)
	Good Behavior Game	(MTFC)
	Guiding Good Choices	(PCIT)
	(I Can Problem Solve)	Reading Recovery
	(Incredible Years)	Schools and Families Education Children (SAFE Children)[5]
	Olweus Bullying Program	Stop Now and Plan (SNAP)
	PALS	Targeted Reading Intervention
	PATHS	(Triple P)
	Planet Health	
	Positive Action	
	Power Teaching Mathematics	
	Project SPARK	
	Quick Reads	
	Roots of Empathy	
	(Success for All)	
	TAI Math	
	The Reading Edge	
	(Triple P)	

	Interventions for all children	Interventions for children in need
Secondary school years	Adolescent Transitions Program	Adolescents Coping with Depression
	All Stars	(Brief Strategic Family Therapy)
	CASASTART	(Bright Bodies)
	(Guiding Good Choices)	Career Beginnings
	(Incredible Years)	Carrera Pregnancy Prevention
	Life Skills Training	(Coping Power)
	Lions Quest Skills for Adolescence	Functional Family Therapy (FFT)
	(Olweus Bullying Program)	(Homebuilders)
	(Planet Health)	(Incredible Years)
	(Positive Action)	(MTFC)
	Power Teaching Mathematics (STAD)	Multi-systemic Therapy (MST)
	Reducing the Risk	Parenting Wisely
	(Roots of Empathy)	Project TND
	Safe Dates	Read 180
	Safer Choices	Shapedown
	STARS for Families	Together Learning Choices (TLC)
	(Success for All)	(Triple P)
	Teen Outreach	Varying Maternal Involvement in a Weight Loss Program
	(Triple P)	
	Youth AIDS Prevention Project	

The following provides brief descriptions of the top tier programmes.

Tier one Programme Overviews

Early literacy and learning model
http://www.unf.edu/dept/fie/ellm-plus-home.html

The Early Literacy and Learning Model (ELLM) is a US literacy-focused curriculum and support system designed for young children from low-income families. The ELLM program includes curriculum and literacy building blocks, assessment for instructional improvement, professional development for literacy coaches and teachers, family involvement, and collaborative partnerships. The ELLM curriculum and support system is designed to enhance existing classroom curricula by specifically focusing on children's early literacy skills and knowledge. The ELLM curriculum materials include a set of literacy performance standards; monthly literacy packets; targeted instructional strategies; resource guides for teachers; a book lending library; and literacy calendars. ELLM requires a two-hour block of daily literacy and language instruction. Trained literacy coaches provide instructional support to preschool teachers who use the curriculum.

Functional Family Therapy
http://www.fftinc.com/

Functional Family Therapy is a structured family-based intervention that works to enhance protective factors and reduce risk factors in the family. FFT has three-phases. The first phase is designed to motivate the family toward change; the second phase teaches the family how to change a specific critical problem identified in the first phase; and the final phase helps the family generalize their problem-solving skills. A randomised controlled trial of Functional Family Therapy is currently underway in Brighton as part of the SAFE Project.

Incredible Years
http://www.incredibleyears.com/Program/incredible-years-series-overview.pdf

The Incredible Years parent training intervention is a series of programs focused on strengthening parenting competencies (monitoring, positive discipline, confidence) and fostering parents' involvement in children's school experiences in order to promote children's academic, social and emotional competencies and reduce conduct problems. The Parent programs are grouped according to age. Babies & Toddlers (0-3 years), BASIC Early Childhood (3-6 years), BASIC School-Age (6-12 years) and ADVANCED (6-12 years). Incredible years has been widely delivered across the UK including delivery with a focus on the disadvantaged through Welsh Sure Start Centres and a 0-12 program being delivered through Manchester's Children and Parents Service.

Life Skills Training
http://www.lifeskillstraining.com/

Life Skills Training (LST) is a school-based classroom intervention to prevent and reduce the use of tobacco, alcohol, and marijuana. Teachers deliver the program to middle/junior high school students in 30 sessions over three years. Students in the program are taught general self-management and social skills and skills related to avoiding drug use.

Let's begin with the letter people
http://www.abramslearningtrends.com/lets_begin_with_letter_people.aspx

Let's Begin with the Letter People is a program designed to enhance early language and literacy skills. The program targets many areas of language development including building letter knowledge, phonological awareness, language and motivation to read, development of vocabulary, and receptive and expressive language development. The Let's Begin program also has a special emphasis on letter knowledge and phonological awareness.

Lion's quest skills for Adolescence
http://www.lions-quest.org/

Lions Quest *Skills for Adolescence* is a schoolwide program designed for middle school students (grades 6–8). The program was designed to promote good citizenship skills, core character values, and social-emotional skills and discourage the use of drugs, alcohol, and violence. The program includes a classroom curriculum, schoolwide practices to create a positive school climate, parent and family involvement, and community involvement. The curriculum may vary in scope and intensity, lasting from nine weeks to three years. The lessons use cooperative group learning exercises and classroom management techniques to improve classroom climate.

The Parent-Child Home Program
http://www.parent-child.org/

The parent-child home programme promotes parent-child interaction and positive parenting to enhance children's cognitive and social-emotional development. The program prepares children for academic success and strengthens families through intensive home visiting. Twice weekly home visits are designed to stimulate the parent-child verbal interaction, reading, and educational play critical to early childhood brain development. Each week the home visitors bring a new book or educational toy that remains with the families permanently. Using the book or toy, home visitors model for parents and children reading, conversation, and play activities that stimulate quality verbal interaction and age-appropriate developmental expectations. The Parent-Child Home Programme has been implemented in Ireland, Bermuda, Canada and the US.

Nurse Family Partnership/Family Nurse Partnership
http://www.nursefamilypartnership.org/

http://www.dh.gov.uk/en/Publicationsandstatistics/Publications/PublicationsPolicyAndGuidance/DH_118530

Nurse Family Partnership provides intensive visitation by nurses during a woman's pregnancy and the first two years after birth; the program was developed by Dr. David Olds. The goal is to promote the child's development and provide support and instructive parenting skills to the parents. The program is designed to serve low-income, at-risk pregnant women bearing their first child. It is being delivered in the UK as Family Nurse Partnership. Department of Health is currently undertaking a number of Randomised Controlled Trials across the UK.

Promoting Alternative Thinking Strategies (PATHS)
http://www.channing-bete.com/prevention-programs/paths/

The PATHS curriculum facilitates the development of self-control, positive self-esteem, emotional

awareness and interpersonal problem solving skills, with an increased vocabulary and understanding of emotions. The programme also focuses on improving empathy for the feelings of others, an understanding of attributional processes and a better understanding of the effects of behaviours. It links with the current PSHE curriculum and works positively to promote whole school behaviour policies.

Multi-Systemic Therapy
http://www.mstservices.com/

Multi-Systemic Therapy (MST) is an intervention for youth that focuses on improving the family's capacity to overcome the known causes of delinquency. Its goals are to promote parents' ability to monitor and discipline their children and replace deviant peer relationships with pro-social friendships. Trained MST therapists, working in teams consisting of one Ph.D. clinician and three or four clinicians with masters' degrees, have a caseload of four to six families. The intervention typically lasts between three and six months. The first randomised controlled trial of MST in the UK run by the Brandon Centre in partnership with Camden and Haringey Youth Offending Services.

Multidimensional Treatment Foster Care
http://www.mtfc.com/index.html

Multidimensional Treatment Foster Care (MTFC) (versus regular group care) is an alternative to group or residential treatment, incarceration, and hospitalization for adolescents with chronic antisocial behavior, emotional disturbance, and delinquency. Community families are recruited, trained, and closely supervised to provide MTFC-placed adolescents with treatment and intensive supervision at home, in school, and in the community. MTFC emphasizes clear and consistent limits with follow-through on consequences, positive reinforcement for appropriate behavior, a relationship with a mentoring adult, and separation from delinquent peers. MTFC is being trialled by Randomised Controlled Trial and Quasi-experimental study in the UK as part of the Care Placements Evaluation.

Start Taking Alcohol Risks Seriously (STARS)
http://wch.uhs.wisc.edu/13-Eval/Tools/Resources/Model%20Programs/STARs.pdf

Start Taking Alcohol Risks Seriously (STARS) for Families is a health promotion program for preventing alcohol use among at-risk middle and junior high school youth (11 to 14 years old). The goal of STARS for Families is to have all youth postpone alcohol use until adulthood. STARS for Families matches media-related, interpersonal, and environmental prevention strategies to each child's specific stages of alcohol initiation, stages of readiness for change, and specific risk and protective factors. This innovative program has been shown to result in avoidance of, or reductions in, alcohol use among participating youth.

Project Toward No Drug Abuse (Project TND)
http://tnd.usc.edu/

Project Towards No Drug Abuse (Project TND) is funded by the National Institute on Drug Abuse as a drug abuse intervention and prevention program for high school-age youth. This school-based program (1) teaches skills, such as healthy coping and self control, (2) educates students about myths and misleading information that encourage substance use and motivates change, (3) warns of chemical dependency and other negative consequences, and (4) provides cessation strategies for those already using drugs. Finally, it encourages youth to use positive decision-making skills, to continue to discuss substance abuse with peers, and to commit to not using substances.

Be Proud! Be Responsible
http://www.etr.org/recapp/index.cfm?fuseaction=pages.ebpDetail&PageID=1

Be Proud! Be Responsible! was developed to lower the prevalence of HIV/AIDS within inner-city, African American communities. The curriculum aims to help young people make "proud and responsible" decisions about their sexual behaviors. This cognitive-behavioral program has repeatedly been shown to have an impact on participants' knowledge of HIV/AIDS and on their attitudes and intentions regarding risky sexual behaviors (such as intentions to use condoms). Furthermore, the program has been shown to reduce sexual activity and decrease sexual partners in adolescent males. Another study found that program participants reported less frequent unprotected sex and were less likely to engage in anal sex. An additional study found that the program increased positive attitudes towards abstinence and self-efficacy regarding the avoidance of unsafe or unwanted sex. Participants were also more likely to talk to parents about issues regarding sex then participants in the control group. This program has not been found to have an impact on whether participants practice abstinence.

Reading Recovery
http://readingrecovery.ioe.ac.uk/

Reading Recovery is an early intervention tutoring programme for pupils aged 6 and 7 who are experiencing difficulty in their beginning reading instruction. The programme provides the lowest achieving readers (lowest 20%) with supplemental tutoring in addition to their normal reading classes. Pupils participating in Reading Recovery receive daily 30-minute one-to-one lessons for 12–20 weeks with a specially trained teacher. The lessons include assessment, reading known stories, reading a story that was read once the day before, writing a story, working with a cut-up sentence, and reading a new book. Reading recovery is a key plank of 'Every Child a Reader'.

Safer Choices
http://www.advocatesforyouth.org/index.php?option=com_content&task=view&id=1128&Itemid=177

Safer Choices is a two-year, school-based, HIV/STI and teen pregnancy prevention program with the primary goal of reducing unprotected sexual intercourse by encouraging abstinence and, among students who report having sex, encouraging condom use. Based on social cognitive theory, social influences theory, and models of social change, Safer Choices is a high school program that includes:

1. A school health protection council;

2. The curriculum;

3. Peer club or team to sponsor school-wide activities;

4. Parenting education; and

5. Links between schools and community-based services.

6. In some schools, programs also incorporate an HIV-positive speaker.

The program is delivered in 20 sequential sessions. Parents receive a newsletter and participate in some student-parent homework assignments. School-community links center on activities to enhance students' familiarity with and access to support services in the community. Each year of the program, schools implement activities across all five components.

Safe dates

http://www.hazelden.org/web/public/safedates.page

Safe Dates is a program designed to stop or prevent the initiation of emotional, physical, and sexual abuse on dates or between individuals involved in a dating relationship. Intended for male and female 8th- and 9th-grade students, the goals of the program include: (1) changing adolescent dating violence and gender-role norms, (2) improving peer help-giving and dating conflict-resolution skills, (3) promoting victim and perpetrator beliefs in the need for help and seeking help through the community resources that provide it, and (4) decreasing dating abuse victimization and perpetration. Safe Dates consists of five components: a nine-session curriculum, a play script, a poster contest, parent materials, and a teacher training outline.

Success for all (including Curiosity Corner)

http://www.successforall.net/index.htm
http://www.successforall.org.uk/

Success for All is a school reform program that focuses on promoting early reading success among educationally at-risk students. The program was developed by Robert Slavin, Nancy Madden, and colleagues at the request of the Baltimore City Public School System, and was piloted in one Baltimore elementary school during the 1987-88 school year. The programme is currently working with over 200 schools in the UK.

Endnotes

1. The evaluation found no effect on boys' attitudes or behaviour regarding pregnancy prevention.

2. For children from low-income families.

3. Under-8s from low-income families.

4. Children aged 1-3 from low-income families.

5. Targeted at 1st grade (US) children in inner-city neighbourhoods.

Annex C
Standards of Evidence Criteria

A. EVALUATION QUALITY

GOOD ENOUGH

A1. One randomised controlled trial OR two quasi-experimental evaluations (initial quasi-experimental evaluation and a replication) with the following characteristics:

Requires evidence of one RCT or two quasi-experimental evaluations in which criteria A1a to A1e are all met. Also requires specification of (a) the process of allocation (random, non-random – and if the latter precisely what this involves), and (b) the groups to which units are allocated (e.g. program, control, placebo, variations on the program).

A1a. Assignment to the intervention should be at a level appropriate to the intervention, i.e. individual, school, etc. (to reduce spill-over effects, etc.)

Requires specification of the unit of allocation (e.g. individual, class, school). For example, if it is a school-based intervention, schools should be assigned to different conditions (not students, or classrooms), if it is a single-site evaluation of a community-based parent training program, families should be assigned to the different conditions.

A1b. Use of measurement instruments that are appropriate for the intervention population of focus and desired outcomes.

Where standardised measures are used it requires specification of (a) the name of the measure (and, where relevant, individual sub-scales) and either (b) reported reliability and validity (using accepted standards e.g. alpha coefficient of 0.70+ and noting the scale

length, and reporting any kappa statistic) or (c) a reference to a suitable source containing that information. Where a 'real-world' or administrative indicator is used (e.g. rates of arrest, detention, school suspension, grade retention) it requires specification of the precise nature of these. In both cases the measure should be appropriate for the construct in question (e.g. the Eyberg Inventory should be used to measure behaviour but not social and emotional learning) and the population to whom it is applied, and there should be no obvious doubts concerning its usefulness. The means of gathering data on the measure in question should be specified (e.g. observation, self-report, interview, archival search, teacher report).

A1c. Analysis based on 'intent-to-treat', meaning all participants in the evaluation are followed-up even when they drop out of the intervention.

Requires evidence that post-test data were collected on participants assigned to both the program and control arms of the evaluation, and that participants assigned to the program arm were treated as such throughout the study. If it was not possible to gather post-test data on all participants and attrition is not too serious it is acceptable for imputation to be used. If attrition is low (under 5%) it can be assumed that the study effectively used an intent-to-treat approach. It is important to note that if randomisation occurs prior to Wave 1/baseline data collection and a subject assigned to a condition does not complete baseline this is a source of attrition i.e. they cannot be eliminated from the evaluation.

A1d. Appropriate statistical analyses.

Requires specification of the methods used to analyse the results, and evidence that these are appropriate given the data being analysed and the purpose of the analysis. For example, the statistical method should be suitable for the type of data used (categorical, ordinal, ratio/ parametric or non-parametric etc.), and should be capable of answering the question of focus (testing differences in averages between groups, or predicting categorical or linear outcomes etc.). If in doubt, concerns about the analyses should be noted. Also, statistical models should control for baseline differences on outcome measures and demographic characteristics.

A1e. Analyses of baseline differences should indicate equivalence between intervention and comparison groups.

A2. There is a minimum of one long-term follow-up (at least 6 months following completion of the intervention) on at least one outcome measure indicating whether results are sustained over time.

Requires evidence that data on the most important outcome measure were collected at least six months after the intervention ended (on both the program and control groups, since the difference must be sustained). In the case of interventions that could in principle be used for many years (e.g. cooperative learning) this criterion will be waived, but it will apply for interventions intended to solve a problem once and for all (e.g. one-to-one tutoring programs). This caveat is likely to apply particularly to educational programs.

A3. There is a clear statement of the demographic characteristics of the population with whom the intervention was tested.

Requires specification of the population with whom the intervention was tested in terms of age, gender, race/ethnicity and socio-economic status.

A4. There is documentation regarding what participants received in the intervention and counterfactual conditions.

Requires specification of what participants received. This should relate as closely as possible to the description given in criterion

C4; that is, if the intervention is delivered as stated there it is sufficient to indicate this, but if there are significant differences in any regard – for example, the intervention is truncated, extended, adapted for cultural or other contextual reasons or delivered by a different set of practitioners – then this should be noted. It should also be specified whether all participants received the same intervention; in some studies there are two or more program groups, with participants in each one receiving a different version of the intervention, in which case this should be indicated.

A5. There is no evidence of significant differential attrition.

Requires specification of (a) the amount of drop-out from both program and control groups in each relevant study, and (b) if and how this varies according to assignment condition, demographic characteristics (age, gender, race/ethnicity, socio-economic status) and/or relevant risk factor/promotive factor/ outcome characteristics of the population targeted. Differential attrition will be considered 'significant' if (a) there is evidence that significantly more participants from either group when compared with the other were lost to post-test or follow-up or if (b) significantly more participants with specific characteristics that could bias apparent results were lost from one group than from the other group.

A6. Outcome measures are not dependent on the unique content of the intervention.

Requires evidence that the measures are not limited specifically to the intervention; that is, they could be used to measure the relevant construct in studies of other interventions seeking the same outcomes. It should be clear that an artificial impression of effectiveness is not created by measuring things that are (a) only addressed by the program in question and (b) not highly relevant outside of that context.

A7. Outcome measures must reflect relevant outcomes.

Requires evidence that one or more of the outcome measures reflects one or more relevant outcomes.

A8. Outcome measures are not rated solely by the person or people delivering the intervention.

Requires evidence that for at least one relevant outcome the measures are not rated solely by the person or people delivering the intervention. For example, a school-based intervention to improve children's behaviour would not meet this criterion if (a) the measure of behaviour relied solely on teacher ratings and (b) those same teachers implemented the intervention.

BEST

A9. There are two RCTs OR one RCT and one quasi-experimental design evaluation (in which analysis and controls rule out plausible threats to internal validity).

Requires evidence that at least two RCTs or one RCT and one quasi-experimental design evaluation were conducted on the intervention in question and, critically, that they meet the criteria outlined in A1 above. The studies need to meet the methodological requirements spelled out in all 'good enough' evaluation quality criteria (A1-A8).

A10. The evaluation results indicate the extent to which fidelity of implementation affects the impact of the intervention.

Requires evidence that the interaction between fidelity of implementation and impact of the intervention on one or more relevant outcomes was analysed. In order for this criterion to be met there does not have to be evidence that a relationship exists – only that the analysis was conducted and reported.

A11. Dose-response analysis is reported.

Requires evidence that (a) there were two or more variations on the program according to the amount of intervention to be delivered, and that these variations were determined prior to the study commencing, and (b) the relationship between the amount of intervention delivered and the relevant outcome(s) is analysed and reported. It is not sufficient for the analysis only to examine post hoc which participants received most of the intervention and whether this is related to relevant outcomes. In order for this criterion to be met there does not have to be

evidence that a relationship exists – only that the analysis was conducted and reported.

A12. Where possible or appropriate there is analysis of the impact on sub-groups (e.g. do the results hold up for different age groups, boys and girls, ethnic minority groups?).

Requires evidence that the impact of the program was considered, where relevant, in relation to different sub-groups defined by demographic characteristics (age, gender, race/ethnicity, socio-economic status) and/or relevant risk factor/promotive factor / outcome characteristics. For example, there might be analysis of whether the program worked better for boys than for girls, or whether children with more serious needs at the outset improved disproportionately. In order for this criterion to be met there does not have to be evidence that a relationship exists – only that the analysis was conducted.

A13. There is verification of the theoretical rationale underpinning the intervention, provided by mediator analysis showing that effects are taking place for the reasons expected.

Requires evidence that (a) a proper mediation analysis was completed, and (b) the mediation analysis demonstrated a mediation effect. It is not sufficient for there to be evidence that the program had an impact on one or more predicted mediators, and one or more designated outcomes, and to conclude therefore that there is a mediation effect. Rather, the analysis must follow Baron & Kenny's four steps: (1) Show that the initial variable (X) is correlated with the outcome (Y); (2) Show that the initial variable (X) is correlated with the mediator (M); (3) Show that the mediator (M) affects the outcome variable (Y); and (4) Test whether M completely or partially mediates the X-Y relationship (if M completely mediates the X-Y relationship then the effect of X on Y controlling for M should be zero).

B. IMPACT

GOOD ENOUGH

B1. There is a positive impact on a relevant outcome.

Requires evidence that in a majority of studies complying with the 'good enough' evaluation quality criteria set out in section A, program group participants did better relative to the control group participants on a relevant outcome, and that the difference is statistically significant. In addition, there should be a statement of (a) the population with whom the program has been demonstrated to be effective, defined in terms of the relevant characteristics outlined in C1, (b) any relevant conditions under which the effectiveness was found to vary (e.g. relating to setting or features of implementation), and (c) any sub-group analyses done and subgroups for which specific positive findings were found (e.g. girls, high risk youth).

B2. There is a positive and statistically significant effect size, with analysis done at the level of assignment (or, if not, with appropriate correction made).

Requires evidence that in one or more studies (a) there is a statistically significant positive difference between the program and control groups (identified in B1), and (b) either an effect size is reported (using Cohen's d) or it is possible to calculate Cohen's d from the data reported, and (c) the analysis was conducted at the level of assignment as specified in criterion A1a or, if it was not, the reason for this has been explained and the appropriate correction made. Effect sizes, or differences in proportions between program and control groups, should be reported, as should the significance levels of those differences. If the effect size is not reported then report the information that would permit it to be calculated. Specifically, (a) in the case of continuous data report the mean and standard deviations for intervention and control groups, and/or (b) in the case of categorical data report the proportion in the category of interest for the intervention and control groups.

OR

There is a reported sample size weighted mean effect size of .2, with a sample size of more than 500 individuals across all studies.

Requires that in one or more studies meeting the A1-A8 criteria, there was a positive effect of at least 20% of the control group's standard deviation, and a total sample size of at least 500 participants. The importance of this requirement is that in many studies with large clusters (such as schools), it is practically impossible to obtain sample sizes large enough to permit analysis at the cluster level, but unbiased and meaningful estimates can be obtained using participant-level analyses when sample sizes at the participant level are large.

B3. There is an absence of iatrogenic effects for intervention participants. (This includes all sub-groups and important outcomes.)

Requires that there be no evidence of the intervention having a harmful effect on participants either as a whole or sub-groups of participants in relation to any of the relevant outcome areas. Evidence of an iatrogenic effect should come from a study or studies that meet the methodological standards required to demonstrate a positive effect; that is, from a study that meets the evaluation quality criteria set out in A1-A8. It is permissible for there to be iatrogenic effects in areas that are not critically important for relevant outcomes (For example, if a program significantly and substantially lowers actual teen pregnancy, it matters less if some attitudes (not behaviours) towards sex are 'worse off' after the intervention. This said, it is helpful to record any evidence of an iatrogenic effect, particularly if it only affects a sub-group (e.g. boys but not girls), because if the program is revised to incorporate this finding it be might decided to recommend the program (i.e. for the group for whom there are positive and no iatrogenic effects). Moreover, where there is a positive effect but some harmful side-effect on another behaviour or attitude this should be reported.

BEST

B4. If two or more RCTs or at least one RCT and one QED have been conducted, and they meet the methodological criteria stipulated in section A (see criterion A9), there is evidence of a positive effect (criterion B1) and an absence of iatrogenic effects (criterion B3) from a majority of the studies.

B5. There is evidence of a positive dose-response relationship that meets the methodological standard stated in A11.

It should be recognized that the relationship may not be linear in the sense that the size of the effect increases in direct proportion to the amount of the program received. For example, the relationship may be curvilinear (e.g. the effect is reasonably constant for participants receiving between 1 and 10 weeks of the program but increases gradually for participants receiving it for 11-13 weeks and then steeply for those receiving more than that). Equally, there may be a threshold effect, whereby there is a relationship up to, say, 10 weeks, at which point the maximum effect is shown, but that it makes little or no difference to the size of effect if participants have received 10 weeks or 30 weeks.

C. INTERVENTION SPECIFICITY

GOOD ENOUGH

C1. Intended population of focus is clearly defined.

Requires evidence for the population of focus of (a) relevant demographic characteristics (age, gender, ethnic group, socio-economic status, urban/rural) and (b) relevant outcome, risk and promotive factor status. It is not necessary for all of these to be mentioned, but any definite inclusion or exclusion criteria must be cited. In the case of universal programs, a statement such as 'whole-school intervention for elementary schools' would be sufficient.

C2. Outcomes of the intervention are clearly specified and meet one of the relevant outcomes.

Requires evidence of the objectives of the intervention in terms of (a) the specific outcomes desired, and (b) the desired direction of change (increase or decrease). It is not necessary to specify the size of the desired change or the period over which that change is expected to become evident. For example, it would be sufficient to state that the intervention seeks to reduce anti-social behaviour among adolescents without adding, say, that a given percentage reduction is sought over two years.

C3. Please identify the risk and promotive factors that the program seeks to change, using the program's logic model or theory explaining why the intervention may lead to better outcomes.

Requires specification of the risk and promotive factors that the intervention is seeking to change in order to achieve the desired outcome(s), and the logical connection between changing these factors and achieving those outcome(s). It must be clear why the intervention or aspects of it will, logically, change the risk and promotive factors and so achieve the desired outcomes. The statement will necessarily elaborate briefly on the hypothesised causes and/or consequences of the problem that is being prevented or addressed

C4. There is documentation about what the intervention comprises.

Requires evidence of what the intervention comprises as designed, focusing on what is provided, by whom, over what period, for how long, with what frequency, where and how. Thus, it is necessary to state (a) the content of the intervention (e.g. information, advice, training, money, advocacy), (b) the nature of the provider (e.g. social worker, teacher, psychologist, volunteer), (c) the duration of the intervention (e.g. 3 hours, 6 weeks, a school year), (d) the length of inputs (e.g. 2 hours), (e) the frequency of inputs (e.g. daily, weekly, monthly), (f) the setting (e.g. school, community centre, health clinic) and (g) the mode of delivery (e.g. group-based, one-to-one). In the case of a multi-component intervention – for example, one that has components for children only, parents only, and also children and parents together – it is necessary for component to be described in these terms.

BEST

C5. There is a research base summarizing the prior empirical evidence to support the causal mechanisms (risk and protective factors) that underlie the change in outcomes being sought.

Requires specification in material produced by the program developer of the extant empirical evidence on (a) the aetiology of the problem that is being prevented or addressed (expressed in terms of risk and promotive factors and relevant outcomes), and (b) how aspects of the intervention have been found in other studies to be successful in changing relevant risk and promotive factors and so achieve the desired outcomes. There should be a statement of the nature and robustness of the research methods used to establish the evidence cited.

D. SYSTEM READINESS

GOOD ENOUGH

D1. There are explicit processes for ensuring that the intervention gets to the right people.

Requires evidence of the means by which the population of focus (as defined in criterion C1) gains access to the intervention (as defined in criterion C4). In the case of a universal program it is sufficient to re-state which children receive the intervention, from whom and where. In the case of a targeted program it is necessary to specify outreach and engagement strategies, relevant access and referral pathways, screening procedures, checks, interviews and so on, indicating what is decided by whom, on what basis and in what sequence.

D2. There are training materials and implementation procedures.

Requires evidence that there are suitable materials used to train practitioners in terms of both what they implement (content) and how they implement it (process).

D3. There is a manual(s) detailing the intervention.

Requires evidence of a manual or series of manuals specifying in detail what the intervention comprises. This will typically include instructions for implementers and/or materials that need to be delivered by implementers to the target population (e.g. lesson plans).

D4. There is reported information on the financial resources required to deliver the intervention.

Requires a description of costs associated with implementing the program, including: start-up costs; intervention implementation costs; intervention implementation support costs, such as technical assistance and training; and costs associated with fidelity monitoring and evaluation. It is not sufficient just to state the total cost, or average cost per participant is: there must be some breakdown along the lines suggested.

D5. There is reported information on the human resources required to deliver the intervention.

Requires a description of the staff resources needed to deliver the intervention, including required staff ratios, the required level of qualifications and skills for staff, and the amount of time they will need to allocate (to cover delivery, training, supervision, preparation and travel).

D6. The program that was evaluated is still available.

Requires evidence that the intervention is currently available for sites wishing to implement it – for example, that it has an up-to-date website and that materials can be ordered.

BEST

D7. The program is currently being widely disseminated.

Requires specification of where (geographically) the program has been implemented, the number of places in which it has been implemented, the number of people served and the period over which these figures apply.

D8. The program has been tested in 'real world' conditions (real staff, real settings), meaning that it was tested in conditions that are replicable and not biasing.

Requires evidence that the program has been tested in conditions that are replicable outside of a funded research study. Look for evidence of researchers having substantially less control in implementing the intervention (although they often remain in charge of training, data collection and analysis), and settings in which (a) some practitioners adhere to treatment manuals and others do not, (b) organizational support waxes and wanes and (c) factors such as policy changes, budget cuts and differential leadership have to be contended with. Put another way, the intervention should have been delivered by real staff (i.e. not people working for the research team), in real settings (i.e. in orthodox service provision venues) and without intensive support from people employed by the research team.

D9. Technical support is available to help implement the intervention in new settings.

Requires specification of the content of support, the medium of provision (e.g. in person, phone) and its frequency and duration. In order for this criterion to be met it is critical that the support is currently and readily available – that is, it actually exists rather than being something in writing only – and that it is available on an ongoing basis as required.

D10. Absolute investment is stated.

Requires specification of how much it costs to implement the intervention in its entirety (i.e. at least one iteration). It must be clear what the cost means in terms of (a) number of staff involved in implementation, (b) number of children and families served, (c) period for which the amount is calculated, and (d) when and where the calculation applies to (year, country). Since costs will vary substantially across implementation sites, as far as possible it would help to report the average cost or range of costs across as many implementations as available. If they add or delete modules in the series of studies or 'replications' please note this as it adds another complication in how we report costs.

D11. There is a fidelity protocol or assessment checklist to accompany the program.

Requires evidence that there is a method for independent monitors to measure implementation fidelity.

Annex D
Evidence of Programmes cost-effectiveness

Programme	Description	Age of children involved	Measured examples of impact, outcomes and cost effectiveness
Nurse Family Partnership/ Family Nurse Partnership	Intensive home visiting programme administered by health professionals. It is delivered to first-time mothers	0-2 Years	NFP has consistently delivered positive economic returns over 30 years of rigorous research. Benefit-to-cost ratios of examined studies fall in the range of around 3:1 to 5:1. Some example impacts from the US evaluation include; Age 2 – Nurse visited children seen in emergency departments 32% fewer times Age 4 – effect on health encounters endured (on average 1 visit per child to emergency room compared to 1.5 for the control Age 15 – greater effects on reports of child abuse than at age 4 (0.29 verified reports vs 0.54 for the control group) – fewer subsequent pregnancies (1.5 vs 2.2 for the control) – fewer months on welfare (60 vs 90 months for the control) – fewer arrests (average of 0.16 vs 0.9 for the control).

Programme	Description	Age of children involved	Measured examples of impact, outcomes and cost effectiveness
Triple P	Multi-tiered parenting program with universal to highly targeted elements	0-16 Years	One of two parenting interventions identified by NICE as cost-effective in reducing conduct disorder. The large lifetime costs associated with conduct disorder, estimated to average £75,000 in milder cases to 225,000 in extreme ones, suggesting even a low success rate would constitute good value for money. Measured outcomes from Triple P include; — Significantly lower levels of conduct problems — Noted clinical changes on behaviour scale (33% vs 13% of children with problems)
Incredible Years	Parenting programme for those with children at risk of conduct disorder	0-12 Years	One of two parenting interventions identified by NICE as cost-effective in reducing conduct disorder. The large lifetime costs associated with conduct disorder, estimated to average £75,000 in milder cases to 225,000 in extreme ones suggest even a low success rate would constitute good value for money. Evaluation outcomes include; — children had significantly reduced antisocial and hyperactive behaviour — reduction in parenting stress and improvement in parenting competencies — positive effects on child behaviour and parenting
Parent Child Interaction Therapy	A Parent-Child intervention designed to improving the quality of the parent-child relationship and change interaction patterns .	2-7 Years	A review of Parent Child Interaction Therapy found it to have a Benefit-to-Cost ratio of around 3.5:1. Improvements noted include; — Improved child behavior — Reduced parental Stress — Reduced abuse and Neglect

Programme	Description	Age of children involved	Measured examples of impact, outcomes and cost effectiveness
Success for All	A range of programmes which foster school readiness and early literacy and numeracy development	3-11 Years	A US economic evaluation found Success for All cost the same to deliver as the control group through reduced need for remedial schooling. For low-acheiving students Success for All was found to notably cheaper – $2600 less, than the standard educational approach. Some example impacts include; – better attainment – fewer special education placements – less frequent grade retentions
Multi-dimensional treatment foster care	A fostering programme where families are recruited, trained, and closely supervised to provide adolescents with treatment and intensive supervision at home, in school, and in the community	3-16 Years	An US economic appraisal of Multi-Dimensional Treatment Foster Care found a benefit to cost ratio of around 11:1. The potential savings from rolling out 8 adolescent units of MDTFC for 5 years have been estimated at £213,500,000 after 7 years, provided assumptions on take up and other factors are met. The latest annual report for England found statistically significant differences on; – Offending – Self-harm – Sexual behaviour problems – Absconding – Fire setting.
PATHS – Promoting Alternative Thinking Strategies	A primary school curriculum for students designed to develop self-control, positive self-esteem, emotional awareness and interpersonal problem solving skills.	4-6 Years	PATHs is relatively low cost programme, estimated at $15-45 in the US. Evaluations of PATHS have found positive impacts on; – Reducing Sadness and Depression – Lower Peer Aggression and Disruptive Behaviour – Improved Classroom Atmosphere

Programme	Description	Age of children involved	Measured examples of impact, outcomes and cost effectiveness
Reading Recovery	Reading Recovery is a school-based, short-term intervention designed for children who are the lowest literacy achievers after their first year of school.	5-6 Years	The benefits of delivering reading recovery, as part of the every child a reader campaign, have been estimated in the range of around £15 to £17 per pound of cost over the period 2006 to 2039. This is based on a range of outcomes, including special educational need provision, crime and health costs.
Life Skills Training	A school-based intervention to developing social skills to prevent alcohol and substance misuse, behavioural problems and risky sexual behaviour	9-15 Years	A US Economic Appraisal of Life Skills Training estimates the Benefit to Cost Ratio at 25:1. A review of alcohol interventions by National Institute of Clinical Excellence noted the impact of LST on long-term drinking behavior. Noted outcomes include reductions in the use of – Tobacco – Drugs – Alcohol.
Functional Family Therapy (FFT)	A structured family-based intervention that works to enhance protective factors and reduce risk factors in the family. This is aimed at youths displaying anti-social behaviour and/or offending	10-17 Years	Functional Family Therapy has been estimated to have a Benefit to Cost ratio of around 7.5:1 to 13:1. Clinical trials have demonstrated impacts on; – Treating adolescents with Conduct Disorder, Oppositional Defiant Disorder, Disruptive Behavior Disorder – Treating alcohol and other drug abuse disorders, and who are delinquent and/or violent – reducing crime – likelihood of entry into the care system.

Programme	Description	Age of children involved	Measured examples of impact, outcomes and cost effectiveness
Multi Systemic Therapy (MST)	A youth intervention that focuses on improving the family's capacity to overcome the known causes of delinquency	12-17 Years	The Benefit to Cost ratio of Multi-systemic therapy has been estimated at around 2.5:1. Noted outcomes from evaluations include; – reductions of 25-70% in long-term rates of rearrest, – reductions of 47-64% in out-of-home placements, – improvements in family functioning – decreased mental health problems for serious juvenile offenders.

References

Nurse Family Partnership/Family Nurse Partnership

Department for Children, Schools and Families, Cost-Benefit Analysis of Interventions with Parents, 2007, Research Report DCSF-RW008

Triple P

Department for Children, Schools and Families, Cost-Benefit Analysis of Interventions with Parents, 2007, Research Report DCSF-RW008

http://guidance.nice.org.uk/TA102/Guidance/Evidence

Centre for Mental Health, Chance of a lifetime: Preventing early conduct problems and reducing Crime, 2009,

Incredible Years

Department for Children, Schools and Families, Cost-Benefit Analysis of Interventions with Parents, 2007, Research Report DCSF-RW008

http://guidance.nice.org.uk/TA102/Guidance/Evidence

Centre for Mental Health, Chance of a lifetime: Preventing early conduct problems and reducing Crime, 2009,

Parent Child Interaction Therapy

S.Aos, R. Lieb, J. Mayfield, M. Miller, & A. Pennucci. (2004) Benefits and costs of prevention and early intervention programs for youth. Olympia: Washington State Institute for Public Policy, Document No. 04-07-3901

Parent-Child Interaction Therapy: An Examination of Cost-Effectiveness. Journal of Early and Intensive Behavioral Intervention, 5(1), 119-132

Success for All

Borman. G, Hewes. G, 2001, The long-term effects and cost-effectiveness of Success for All, Report 53, Center for Research on the Education of Students Placed At Risk

Borman G & Hewes G, "The long-term effects and cost-effectiveness of Success for All", Educational Evaluation and Policy Analysis, 24 (4), 243-266, 2002

Multi-dimensional treatment foster care

Multidimensional Treatment Foster Care in England, Annual Project Report, 2010
http://www.mtfce.org.uk/reports/MTFCE%206th%20Annual%20Progress%20Report%202010%20Final2.pdf

PATHS – Promoting Alternative Thinking Strategies

http://www.colorado.edu/cspv/blueprints/modelprograms/PATHS.html, 2006

Schools and Families Educating Children (SAFE Children)

Tolan P, Gorman-Smith D, Henry D and Schoeny M (2010) The benefits of booster interventions: evidence from a family-focused prevention program, Prevention Science, 10, (4), 287-297

Reading Recovery

KPMG foundation, The long-term cost of Literacy Difficulties, 2006,
http://www.kpmg.co.uk/pubs/ECR2006.pdf

Life Skills Training (LST)

S.Aos, R. Lieb, J. Mayfield, M. Miller, & A. Pennucci. (2004) Benefits and costs of prevention and early intervention programs for youth. Olympia: Washington State Institute for Public Policy, Document No. 04-07-3901

Jones. L, James. M, Jefferson. T, Lushey. C, Morleo. M, Stokes. E, Sumnall. H, Witty. K, Bellis.M, A review of the effectiveness and cost-effectiveness of interventions delivered in primary and secondary schools to prevent and/or reduce alcohol use by young people under 18 years old, 2007, National Institute of Clinical Excellence

Functional Family Therapy (FFT)

S.Aos, R. Lieb, J. Mayfield, M. Miller, & A. Pennucci. (2004) Benefits and costs of prevention and early intervention programs for youth. Olympia: Washington State Institute for Public Policy, Document No. 04-07-3901

http://www.colorado.edu/cspv/blueprints/ modelprograms/FFT.html, 2007

Multi Systemic Therapy (MST)

S.Aos, R. Lieb, J. Mayfield, M. Miller, & A. Pennucci. (2004) Benefits and costs of prevention and early intervention programs for youth. Olympia: Washington State Institute for Public Policy, Document No. 04-07-3901

http://www.colorado.edu/cspv/blueprints/ modelprograms/MST.html, 2006

Annex E
Evidence-based Practice Databases

Database Name	Web Address	Type of programs covered
BEE (Best Evidence Encyclopedia)	http://www.bestevidence.org/	Educational program including math and reading programs, comprehensive school reform programs and early childhood education programs
California Evidence-Based Clearinghouse for Child Welfare	http://www.cebc4cw.org/	Child welfare programs
CDC Prevention Strategies database	http://www.cdc.gov/prc/prevention-strategies/index.htm	Community health
Center for the Study of Violence Prevention, Blueprints for Violence Prevention	http://www.colorado.edu/cspv/blueprints/	Violence, drug, and crime prevention programs
CASEL Safe and Sound	http://www.casel.org/programs/selecting.php	Programs that support children's social and emotional learning
Child Trends/LINKS Database	http://www.childtrends.org/Links/	Out-of-school time programs that work to enhance children's development
Coalition for Evidence-Based Policy	http://evidencebasedprograms.org/wordpress/	Broad range of programs from early childhood to employment and welfare

Database Name	Web Address	Type of programs covered
Communities that Care	http://depts.washington.edu/sdrg/DASAmeet4-07.pdf http://download.ncadi.samhsa.gov/Prevline/pdfs/ctc/CTC%20Prevention%20Strategies%20Guide%20_pdf.pdf	Programs that address at least one risk or protective factor associated with substance abuse, delinquency, teen pregnancy, school drop-out or violence
Department of Health and Human Services/ Pregnancy Prevention Research Evidence Review	http://www.hhs.gov/ophs/oah/prevention/research/programs/index.html	Teen pregnancy prevention
Penn State Prevention Research Center's EPIS Center	http://www.episcenter.psu.edu/?q=ebp	Delinquency, violence, and substance use and promote positive youth development
Evidence for Policy and Practice Information and Co-ordinating Centre, at the Social Science Research Unit, Institute of Education, University of London	http://eppi.ioe.ac.uk/cms/Default.aspx?tabid=185	Includes databases on health and education
Evidence-Based Program Directory on FindYouthinfo.gov	http://findyouthinfo.gov/DefaultSearch.aspx?sc=Pr	Youth programs
Mathematica publications	http://www.mathematica-mpr.com/publications	Employment programs
National Institute of Drug Abuse, Examples of research-based drug abuse prevention programs	http://www.nida.nih.gov/Prevention/examples.html	Programs that prevent drug use for youth
National Registry of Evidence-based Programs and Practices)	http://www.nrepp.samhsa.gov/	interventions for the prevention and treatment of mental and substance use disorders
Office of Juvenile Justice and Delinquency Prevention Model Programs Database	http://www2.dsgonline.com/mpg/Default.aspx	A comprehensive database of youth programs

Database Name	Web Address	Type of programs covered
Out-of-school time program evaluation and research database	http://www.hfrp.org/out-of-school-time/ost-database-bibliography/database	Out of school time programs
Promising Practices Network	http://www.promisingpractices.net/programs.asp	Programs shown to have outcomes for children, including some family support and parent education programs.
Partnership for Results	http://www.partnershipforresults.org/programs.html	School-based and after school programs for children and families
Strengthening Families	http://www.strengtheningfamilies.org	Effective family programs for preventing juvenile delinquency
Surgeon General	http://www.surgeongeneral.gov/library/youthviolence/toc.html	Prevention and early intervention with youth violence
What Works Clearinghouse	http://ies.ed.gov/ncee/wwc/	Education programs
Wisconsin Clearinghouse on Prevention Resources	http://wch.uhs.wisc.edu/01-Prevention/01-Prev-EvidenceBased-matrix.html	

Annex F
Consultation

Formal responses to the Review's call for evidence were received from:

4Children

a4e

Action for Children

Action in Rural Sussex

Adams, Dr Cheryll

Addaction

Adur & Worthing Council

Alder Hey Children's NHS Foundation Trust

Anna Freud Centre

Antidote

Association of Child Psychotherapists

Auditory Processing Disorder in the UK

Balbernie, Robin

Bangor University

Barnardo's

Bath & North East Somerset Council

Bath & North East Somerset PCT

Beatbullying

Betsi Cadwaladr University Health Board, Wales NHS

Birmingham City Council

Birmingham Community NHS Trust

Blackpool Council

Booktrust

Bottomley MP, Peter

Bristol Community Family Trust

Bromley Children Project

Brook

C4EO

Care for the Family

Catch 22

Centre for Confidence & Well-being

Chance UK

Child Accident Prevention Trust

Child Action North West

Child Maintenance & Enforcement Commission

Child Safety Education Coalition

Children & Parents Service Early Intervention Manchester

Children & Young People's Mental Health Coalition

Children are Unbeatable! Alliance

Children England

Children North East Fathers Plus

Children our Ultimate Investment UK

Children's Centre Committee

Children's Communication Coalition

Children's Rights Alliance for England

City of Bradford Metropolitan District Council

City of Westminster

City Year London

Communication Trust

Concateno TrichoTech

Connexions

Consortium for Emotional Well-being in Schools

Consumer Financial Education Body

ContinU Trust

Coram

Credit Action

Department for Education

Department for Education

Devon County Council

Dialogics Ltd

Dollywood Foundation UK

Early Intervention & Prevention

Early Years

Economic & Social Research Council

Eileen Murphy Consultants & Associates

Elizabeth Jarman

End Violence Against Women Coalition

Enthusiasm Trust

Families in Difficulties

Family & Parenting Institute

Family Action

Family Care

Family Education Development Trust

Family Links

Family Nurse Partnership

Family Planning Association

Family Rights Group

Gosport Voluntary Action

Government Office for the North West

Greater London Authority

Greater Manchester Residuary Body

Greenhouse

Hemel East Ring Of Extended Schools

Hemming MP, John

Homerton Hospital NHS Trust

Home-Start UK

HT Counselling

I CAN

ICE

Imperial College London

Impetus Trust

Incredible Years Inc, Seattle

Independent Commission on Youth Crime & Anti-Social Behaviour

Institute of Education

Interest Group for Parenting and Family Support

Janet Coppola

Kings College London

Kirklees Council

L&Q Housing Association

Learning South West

Leeds City Council

Leslie MP, Chris

LexiaUK Ltd

Libby Colman

Links UK,

London Borough of Barking & Dagenham

London Borough of Barnet

London Borough of Croydon

London Borough of Enfield

London Borough of Hounslow

London Borough of Islington

London Borough of Lambeth

London Borough of Redbridge

London Borough of Tower Hamlets

London School of Economics

London Youth

MAB Consulting

Madeline Barrington-Amat

Manchester City Council

Maypole Children's Centre

Mencap

Mental Health Network

Mentor Foundation UK

Mentoring and Befriending Foundation

Metropolitan Police

Ministry of Justice

Montessori St Nicholas

National Academy for Parenting Research

National Association for People Abused in Childhood

National Association of Independent Schools & Non-Maintained Special Schools

National Childminding Association

National Children's Bureau

National College for Leadership of Schools and Children's Services

National Day Nurseries Association

National Mental Health Development Unit

National Portage Association

National Society for the Protection of Children

National Strategies

Netmums

Newcastle City Council

Newcastle PCT

NHS Croydon

NHS Grampian

NHS Great Yarmouth and Waveney

NHS Nottingham City

NHS South of Tyne and Wear Community Health Services

Norfolk Community Health & Care NHS Trust

North Lancashire NHS Trust

Northumberland Care Trust NHS

Nottingham City Council

Nottinghamshire County Council

Nottinghamshire Domestic Violence Forum

Oadby & Wigston Borough Councils

O'Donnell, Su

Ofsted

One Plus One

One to One Coaches

Oxford Brookes University

Oxford University

Oxfordshire County Council

Parent Infant Clinic and School of Infant Mental Health

Parenting UK

Parentline Plus

Parents as First Teachers

Parents 1st

Partnership for Children

Peach

Pen Pych Community Primary School

Pre-School Learning Alliance

Preventing Youth Offending Project

Private Equity Foundation

Prof Colwyn Trevarthen

PSHE Association

Puzzle Centre

Recro Consulting

Relate

Rochdale Metropolitan Borough Council Youth Service

Rose Hill Children's Centre

RoSPA

Royal College of Psychiatrists

Royal College of Speech & Language Therapists

Royal National Institute for the Blind

Ruane MP, Chris

Save the Children

School Food Trust

School-Home Support

Sense

Services for Children & Young People,

Shropshire County Council

Shropshire County PCT

Signs for Success

Sing and Grow UK

Sloane Court Clinic

Solihull CAMHS

Somerset County Council

South London & Maudsley NHS Foundation Trust

South Lowestoft Children's Centres

South Tyneside PCT

Southwark PCT

Stafford shire County Council

St Giles Trust

Sue Korda

Suffolk County Council

Swindon Borough Council

Tameside & Glossop Early Attachment Service

Tavistock & Portman NHS Trust

Tavistock Centre for Couple Relationships

Teenage Pregnancy Independent Advisory Group

Teenage Pregnancy& Young Parents Services

The British Education Support Trust

The British Psychological Society

The Caspari Foundation

The Centre for Mental Health

The Children's Society

The Deighton Centre

The Dove Service

The Learning Trust

The Lighthouse Group

The Ministry of Parenting Community Interest Company

The Nurture Group Network

The Pillars of Parenting

The Place2Be

The Pupil Parent Partnership

The School & Family Works Ltd

THRIVEftc Associate: Early Years

Together for Children

Training and Development Agency

Trelya

Unite the Union

University of Glasgow

University of London

University of New South Wales

University of Northampton

University of Nottingham

University of Warwick

University of Wolverhampton

U-Too Community Business Ltd

Video Interaction Guidance

Volunteer Centre Sutton

Wakefield District PCT

Warwick University

Warwickshire County Council

Washington State University

West Midlands Fire Service

Westminster City Council

 Wirral Borough Council

Wyre Forest & Hagley Project

YMCA Training

Young Minds

Young Mums and Dads To Be

Young People in Focus

Youth Access

Youth Justice Board

Annex G
Guide to creating a system-ready evidence-based programme

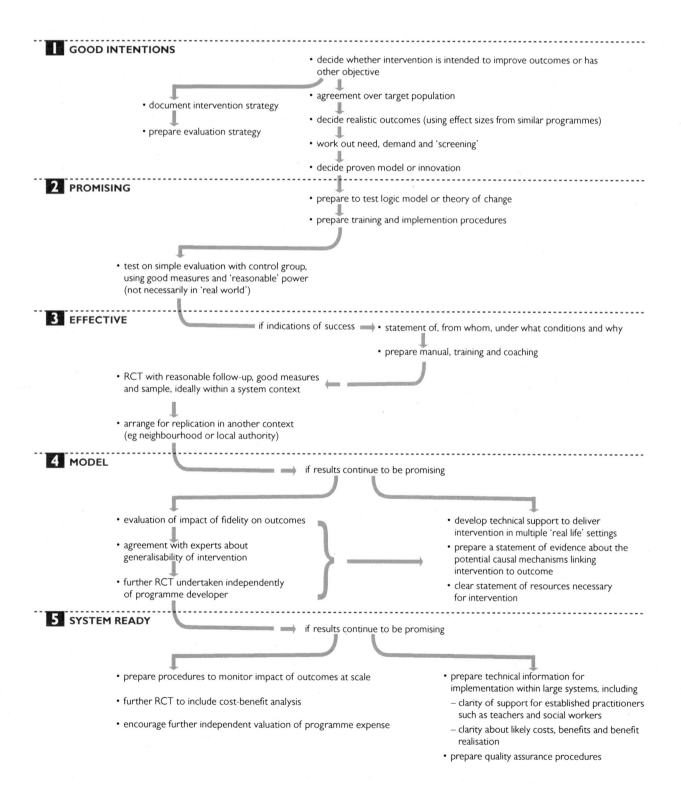

1 GOOD INTENTIONS

- decide whether intervention is intended to improve outcomes or has other objective
- agreement over target population
- document intervention strategy
- decide realistic outcomes (using effect sizes from similar programmes)
- prepare evaluation strategy
- work out need, demand and 'screening'
- decide proven model or innovation

2 PROMISING

- prepare to test logic model or theory of change
- prepare training and implemention procedures
- test on simple evaluation with control group, using good measures and 'reasonable' power (not necessarily in 'real world')

3 EFFECTIVE

if indications of success → • statement of, from whom, under what conditions and why

- prepare manual, training and coaching
- RCT with reasonable follow-up, good measures and sample, ideally within a system context
- arrange for replication in another context (eg neighbourhood or local authority)

4 MODEL

if results continue to be promising

- evaluation of impact of fidelity on outcomes
- agreement with experts about generalisability of intervention
- further RCT undertaken independently of programme developer

- develop technical support to deliver intervention in multiple 'real life' settings
- prepare a statement of evidence about the potential causal mechanisms linking intervention to outcome
- clear statement of resources necessary for intervention

5 SYSTEM READY

if results continue to be promising

- prepare procedures to monitor impact of outcomes at scale
- further RCT to include cost-benefit analysis
- encourage further independent valuation of programme expense

- prepare technical information for implementation within large systems, including
  - clarity of support for established practitioners such as teachers and social workers
  - clarity about likely costs, benefits and benefit realisation
- prepare quality assurance procedures

Support from party leaders for Early Intervention

"I warmly welcome Graham Allen's report on Early Intervention. This government is strongly committed to improving the life chances of every child, but especially those who come from troubled backgrounds. Our plans for early intervention will only succeed if they are based on robust evidence of what works. That is why Graham's report is so useful, because it provides a rigorous framework for assessing which programmes make a difference and then gives clear and practical advice about where taxpayers' money can be most effectively spent. I look forward to the launch of Graham's next report, which will look at how we can go beyond state funding and develop innovative means to finance a growing and proven set of Early Intervention programmes."

Rt Hon David Cameron MP , Prime Minister and Leader of the Conservative part

"The foundations of a fairer, more socially mobile society are laid in the critical early years of life. Parents, communities and government agencies all have a role to play in ensuring that our children have the capabilities they need to prosper and grow. This report by Graham Allen provides plenty of food for thought. But it is also a call for action – the action need to ensure that every child in Britain can realise their full potential"

Rt Hon Nick Clegg MP, Deputy Prime Minister and Leader of the Liberal Democrat party

"At a time when opportunities for young people and social mobility are of huge concern to so many, this report is incredibly timely. Graham has demonstrated very powerfully how parents and children need support from the very earliest years to ensure that all children – regardless of their background – have opportunities to flourish and succeed. That is why new and established forms of public and private sector investment in Early Intervention are so important. I welcome this independent report, its backing for past achievements, its call for future progress and above all the importance it places on expanding the Early Intervention approach to improve children's lives."

Rt Hon Ed Miliband MP, Leader of the Labour Party